Wild Form,
Savage Grammar

Books by Andrew Schelling

Claw Moraine *(1987)*
Ktaadn's Lamp *(1991)*
Dropping the Bow: Poems from Ancient India *(1991)*
Moon is a Piece of Tea *(1991)*
For Love of the Dark One: Songs of Mirabai *(1993, revised 1998)*
The India Book: Essays & Translations from Indian Asia *(1993)*
Two Immortals *(1994)*
Old Growth: Poems & Notebooks 1986-1994 *(1995)*
Songs of the Sons & Daughters of Buddha
WITH ANNE WALDMAN *(1996)*
The Cane Groves of Narmada River:
Erotic Poems from Old India *(1998)*
The Road to Ocosingo *(1998)*
The Handful of Seeds *(1999)*
Tea Shack Interior: New & Selected Poetry *(2001)*
Wild Form Savage Grammar*(2003)*

Editor
Disembodied Poetics: Annals of The Jack Kerouac School
WITH ANNE WALDMAN *(1994)*

WILD FORM
SAVAGE GRAMMAR

Poetry, Ecology, Asia

Andrew Schelling

LA ALAMEDA PRESS   ALBUQUERQUE

My thanks to the editors of the following journals and magazines,
in which earlier versions of these essays have been published:
*Bombay Gin, City Lights Journal, Dark Ages Clasp the Daisy Root, intent, Jacket,
Manoa, New American Writing, The Poetry Project Newsletter, The Robinson Jeffers
Newsletter, Shambhala Sun, Sulfur, Talisman*, and *Tricycle: The Buddhist Journal*.
Also the following publishing houses:
Broken Moon Press, City Lights Books, O Books, Pleasure Boat Studios,
Rodent Press, and Talon Books.

"Wandering Clouds" © adapted from the Introduction to
The Clouds Should Know Me By Now: Buddhist Poet Monks of China,
with permission of Wisdom Publications,
199 Elm St., Somerville, MA 02144   www.wisdompubs.org

"Ramprasad Sen's Poems to the Goddess" adapted from the Forward to
Grace and Mercy in Her Wild Hair: Selected Poems to the Mother Goddess,
with permission of Hohm Press, PO Box 2501, Prescott, AZ 86302.

ISBN: 1-888809-35-3

Library of Congress Cataloging-in-Publication Data

Schelling, Andrew.
  Wild form, savage grammar : poetry, ecology, Asia / Andrew Schelling.
    p. cm.
  ISBN 1-888809-35-3 (alk. paper)
  I. Title.

PS3569.C4796W55 2003
304.2—dc21

2003000669

La Alameda Press
9636 Guadalupe Trail NW
Albuquerque, New Mexico 87114

Contents

Author's Note
30,000 years after Chauvet

———

THESE ESSAYS were mostly written in response to current debates around ecology, wilderness, and wildlife, with an eye out for directives from some vivid old poetries. The United States has more undeveloped public land than any other nation so it makes sense that North Americans are joined and divided by heated biodiversity and wild land discussions. What may seem unexpected is to bring poetry, especially old Asia's, into the mix.

I wrote almost everything here after May 1st, 1990, a date energetically promoted in North America as Earth Day. The mainstream media celebrated the moment as a rekindling of environmental awareness, supposedly dormant for a decade. Eco-activists, narrowing their eyes, regarded the public pronouncements more cynically: the day the major corporations "came out" Green, hoping to usurp the efforts of grass root environmental advocacy groups and anti-nuclear organizations. At a downtown street fair in Berkeley, one prominent booth—maybe the largest—publicized Pacific Gas & Electric's eco-consciousness. Colorful posters showed power plants delicately propped alongside wetlands or backed by conifer forests, untroubled wildlife grazing under the power lines. A street theater troop had meanwhile pulled up a float in front: an eight foot high charcoal colored plaster of Paris nuclear power plant, flashing, rumbling, and belching fumes of dry ice, while black robed figures in death masks scrabbled about in mock worship.

At the University that night Robert Hass and Gary Snyder read poetry to a small Earth Day crowd. Gary made a good challenging remark: That you could not have predicted the emergence of an ecology movement by studying 2000 years of Western metaphysics.

Walking home after the reading, I wondered, could you find roots of an ecology movement in the metaphysics (or literature) of some other culture—India or China? Might excavations in poetry turn up traces of an intellectual lineage capable of augmenting—or at least lending companionship to—the efforts of ecological resistance groups in the West, groups which have gratifyingly come to mix professional and blue collar members, as well as anarchists, bohemians, and Greens?

Much in this book is a response to that challenge. I had first traveled India and the Himalayas in 1973. Returning to North America—to California—I started to study Asian languages and literatures methodically, and have returned to Asia on fact-finding excursions and literary pilgrimages. Too much of contemporary Asia, India in particular, is ecological wreckage. Years of colonial pillaging and deforestation, current population pressures, institutionalized corruption at all levels, and rapid industrialization have staggered the continent. But in regional pockets and in many durable lovely texts there persist fragments of an archaic, nearly forgotten contract between humans and other life forms—a contract that seems to have been circulating since the Paleolithic. Insights from the old contract are retrievable through art and philosophy; some may prove surpassingly practical.

Where would the earliest master artists stand on this? There is the captivating Ice Age bestiary of the people who painted the Chauvet Cave murals—the oldest known paintings—in southern France slightly more than 30,000 years ago. Our artistic peers, those hunters and keen observers of zoological diversity knew a great deal about the wild orders. They and their later colleagues at dozens of sites in the Dordogne and the Pyrenees made paintings the equal in vitality and technical excellence of anything since—mostly of the big animals of their day. The Lion Panel and the Panel of Horses, thundering in charcoal and ochre at Chauvet, are likely to provoke a revaluation of human history in upcoming decades. Jean Clottes, the French Ministry of Culture official who curates the Paleolithic caves, writes that the work of the Chauvet artists, "is not simply regional or national but in fact belongs to all humanity." What was the song, story, and poetry of those early homo sapiens like?

Probably more traces remain in circulation than anyone knows.

What the archaic traditions (and their echoes in Asia, Native America and elsewhere) might come to mean for a nature literate people of today and the future is very exciting. A way out of the West's goofy pastoralism? Out of the neo-Victorian nature writing which dominates the commercial nature magazines? Let's envision somewhere in the immediate future a tradition grander than Romantic landscape verse or regional painting, and far more heartening than nostalgia for a pre-industrial or pre-agricultural past. What might it look like? Could there be a future in which ecology and art fruitfully interact, inspired by biological discoveries and scarcely envisioned conservation sciences of eras to come? My hope is that projective forms of writing will move quickly past visual descriptions of natural phenomena, to enact or recuperate what Aldo Leopold observed to be the grand theaters of ecology and the epic journeys of evolution.

So 30,000 years after Chauvet is such an art possible?

The native habitat of these essays, as of much writing by dear comrades noted in the book, is the small press and its little magazines. Leslie Scalapino's O Books, Clayton Eshleman's *Sulfur*, Ed Foster's *Talisman*, and The Jack Kerouac School of Disembodied Poetics' *Bombay Gin*, to name four, have kept open the migratory routes of good literature. They and many others have done so despite the monstrous consolidation of publishing and book selling into the hands of a few corporate conglomerates. Small presses have been and remain to this day the sharp-eyed, hard working conservators of *wild form*—a term lifted from Jack Kerouac's letters.

May our children and their children's children into the trembling future find cause to enjoy watersheds, bioregions, and grammars that are tawny, playful, wild, bright, and savage.

ANDREW SCHELLING

Boulder, Colorado

July 2002

NOTE ON SPELLING

This book contains a number of Sanskrit words and names. I have generally spelt them with the diacritical marks used by scholars. Having wandered around inside the language twenty-odd years it seems the respectful way to go. Each sound and each letter is traditionally understood as the abode of a deity. Some terms however, particularly place names, have quietly slipped into American speech. I decided to leave Himalayas and Rajasthan as readers of newspapers meet them, without the marks. Likewise a few of the more familiar book titles and honorifics: Isha Upanishad, Mahatma, Maharaja, Shakyamuni.

A.S

A Grammar

Henry David Thoreau, 31 August 1851—his Journal—

*I have no objection to giving the name of some Naturalists—men
of flowers to plants—if by their lives they have identified themselves
with them. There may be a few Kalmias— But it must be done very
sparingly or rather discriminatingly— And no man's name be used
who has not been such a lover of flowers— that the flowers
themselves may be supposed thus to reciprocate his love.*

Out of tantric India from the hands of scholar-adepts come anatomical
ink & paint drawings in which a man or woman's body is displayed—not
inwardly vibrant with physiological organs, but coursing with seed syllables & mystical phrases—the whole constitution, arms, legs, torso, sex
glands, skullpan, comprised of vivid & legible letters carefully inscribed.
This I would take as model of what a man or woman "of letters" might
be—not some bookish habit only—but the body thrill'd so decisively with
language—the person of letters thrilled with an almost sexual delight in
the flush of graphemes like bristling body hair. An indifferent observer
might halt startled at some rippling under the surface. Instead of muscle &
musk a woman perfect in sound & syllable. We might discern as Thoreau
did—"men of flowers"

> stargazing men—
> men of tools—women of fabric—
> of trees, birds—automobile women—
> men of money, children of song.

Today with pensive eye, I sit by a window over tea. November sun tinges the eastern clouds, charcoal & rouge. Man of tea, man of maps, man of sedimentary rock. Man caught back on his own tongue—

He salts the grammars with etymologies
                    to carry in a fur scrotum pouch.
Man of grammar
of poems carved into birch staffs, littered among twig & bark,
clothed in leather or rags,
        man who lifts speech
                    from geologies, brisk mammals, tender grimoires,
        from old loves,
        man of Buckskin Pass, Bear Peak,
        of the two Arapahoes,
                        man of books,
                man of flowers.

Hung in the Mongolia show traveling through Denver is a framed piece of canvas, geometrically drafted by a skilled hand in charcoal, laid over with a swift blush of rouge pigment.

Iconometric Drawing of the Diamond Sow Buddha, Vajravarahī.

An accompanying note attributes it to the painter Luvsanbaldan, early 20th century, who has caged his subject within an architectural grid.

Vajravarahī dances, left foot lifted into her crotch, her body so wild & utterly controlled it's more feral than human. Gaze fixed to the onlooker, she cradles a *khatvanga* staff topped with human skulls in the crook of her left elbow. Buck naked except the magic thread of protection that drops over her spherical breasts. From her headdress the profile of an old angry sow snarls upwards, snout curled on wolf teeth. Tiny calligraphied words in Mongolian script adorn as though gold links & henna tattoos the exposed flesh of Vajravarahī's body.

Spells & syllables on her foot-sole, ankle, knee,
    a phrase inside the taut thigh, over one nipple—
        script on her belly,
    script on her shoulder, her throat—
            mouth & nose.

One delicate word curls along the lip of her prominent vulva.

Jātaka Mind

Originally delivered as a talk at The Jack Kerouac School of Disembodied Poetics, The Naropa Institute, in June 1990, and dedicated to Judi Bari. Two weeks earlier, on May 24th, the Subaru carrying eco-activists Judi Bari and Derryl Cherney exploded as it left Oakland for a Redwoods Summer demonstration. Bari, the driver, was permanently crippled by the pipe bomb placed under her seat. No one has ever been arraigned for the crime.

> Of course we are afraid the children will
> overhear us. But someday someone will overhear
> the children…
> —GEORGE OPPEN, from a letter

IN A FORMER LIFE, *aeons ago, the Buddha took up residence in a forest hermitage. He lived the rigorous life of a recluse, practicing austerities and studying with a resolute mind. One spring day he took some time to saunter through the forest, admiring the wild foliage and attending the songs of birds. He rounded a bend near a mountain crevasse and saw in the cliff wall a cave. There at the mouth of the cave only a few feet from him lay a starving tigress who had just given birth. The tigress was so overcome by her labors and so weakened by hunger she could scarcely move. The future Buddha observed the dark hollows of her eyes. He could see each rib distending the hide over her belly. Starved and confused, she had turned on her whelps, on her own tiger pups, seeing them only as meat to allay the pain of her hunger. The pups, not aware of the danger, had sidled up and were pawing for her teats.*

The future Buddha was overcome by horror. For his own safety he had no thought; it was seeing another sentient creature in distress that made him tremble like a quake in the Himalayas. He thought with despair, "How futile this round of birth and death! The world's vanity is hopeless! In front of my eyes hunger forces a creature to transgress the laws of kinship and affection. She is about to feed on her own tiger cubs. I must get her some food."

But the next instant another thought rose. "Why take meat from some other liv-
ing creature? That would only perpetuate the round of pain and suffering. Here is
my own body, enough meat to feed the tigress. Frail, impure, an ungrateful thing—
mere vehicle of suffering—I can make this body a source of nourishment for an-
other! Only a fool would fail to grasp this opportunity. By doing so may I acquire
the power to release all creatures from misery!"

Climbing a high ridge, he tossed himself down in front of the tigress. On
the verge of slaughtering her pups, hearing the disturbance, she looked across, saw
the fresh corpse, bounded over and ate it. She and her cubs were saved.

THE *Jātaka Tales*, from which this story comes, gather some of the earliest
and strangest stories preserved in the Buddhist heritage. The word *jātaka*
means birth. The old collection which uses the term for its title, and which
must have passed around India in oral form for nearly four hundred years
after the death of the Buddha, was finally committed to writing in about 80
BCE. Scholars set it in Pali, the vernacular language in which all the early
Buddhist texts were set down. The collection preserves five hundred fifty
legends, each recounting one of the Buddha's miraculous former lives in
the aeons before he attained enlightenment. The stories occur in a simple,
rough-hewn prose, studded with cryptic shards of verse that appear to date
from a much earlier period. It is in these broken oddments of poetry that
the oldest trace of a tradition of animal tales is preserved. In all likelihood
the verse fragments are direct carriers of thought from Paleolithic times.

Folklore and archaeology suggest that the *Jātaka Tales'* fascination with
wild animal personalities is by no means an isolated instance. The earliest
evidence of human image making largely depicts animals. Cave art of the
Aurignacian and Magdalenian period, famously found in Spain and southern France, extending from about 32,000 BP (Before Present) to 10,000
years ago (end of the last glaciation), is comprised almost exclusively of
animals. It's store of images contains the region's megafauna or large mammals, but instances of bird life and aquatic creatures also occur. There is every reason to suspect that the earliest verbal art circulating among humans
was concerned with similar themes.

I believe, however, that the *Jātaka Tales* register the first sustained moment in written literature of what I'd call *cross-species compassion*: an imme-

diate and unqualified empathy shown towards creatures not of one's own biological species. Could it be that the tales retain traces of a universal contract between living creatures? A contract so long vanished that no one remembers its distant imperative?

Regarded as written documents the *Jātaka* are quite old, but from an anthropological perspective they look comparatively recent. The physiology of homo sapiens has altered very little in the last hundred thousand years, and through that period all have had the capacity for speech. Some paleontologists suspect Neanderthal also had the capacity to speak. It is certain that the sort of fable preserved in the *Jātaka* occurred many places over long stretches of time. They have survived into our times largely in places like India, where the oral lore of preliterate cultures somehow managed to meet the scholar's pen without too much disruption.

Stories like the one of the Buddha and the tigress reveal a notion of kinship that sweeps across animal species. What's interesting about the *Jātaka Tales*, which carry many traces of archaic human concerns, is that the concern of the storyteller stays with the animals and the biological details are largely accurate. This differentiates them from allegories and other, later tale-types, where animals are transparent stand-ins for humans or human states of mind. Moreover, animals in the *Jātakas* justify the storyteller's interest by consistently showing themselves to be the curators of an ethical order equal to that of humans, often higher.

A thousand, two thousand, maybe ten thousand years after these tales first began to circulate through the villages of South Asia and pass along the trade routes through inner Asia, Mahāyāna Buddhism cast the *Jātaka Tales* into philosophical form. *The Diamond Sūtra* (ca. 2000 years ago), a central document for all of Northern Buddhism, makes explicit what the old stories had gestured towards. In what has come to be known as the "Bodhisattva's vow" the Buddha announces an unqualified interdependence of creatures.

> . . . one should produce a thought in this manner: As many beings as exist in the universe, who can be known by the notion of being—egg-born, born from a womb, born from moisture, or miraculously born;

with form, without form; with perception, without perception, with neither perception nor non-perception—any creature that can possibly be conceived, all these I must lead out of misery, into that realm where occurs no sense of a separate being.

Fashioned somewhere in Northern India during an exuberant period of philosophy, the Bodhisattva vow captures the ethical imperative of Buddhism. India however has passed both metaphysics and ethics down through the ages by draping them in a profuse and nearly hallucinogenic array of symbols. Myth, storytelling, dance, sculpture, music, painting—all have made sophisticated doctrine available to people not trained in the recondite language of metaphysics. It makes sense then that the finest poem to emerge from Buddhist India, a poem that cast Buddhism's metaphysics into durable shape, was a stately re-casting of the ancient *Jātaka Tales*. In about the year 400 the Sanskrit poet Āryaśūra composed his *Jātaka-Mālā*.

Mālā means garland, sometimes necklace, a string of prayer beads or of gemstones. By extension it comes to mean a string of verses or stories. A jātaka-mālā is a garland of birth stories. In polished literary Sanskrit Āryaśūra recounted thirty-three birth stories of the Buddha. They are his versions which appear on the astonishing frescos in the Ajanta Caves near Bombay (bringing the tradition of cave painting down into very recent times); his versions adorn the *stūpa* or reliquary at Sanchi, outside of Banaras. They are also Āryaśūra's versions which appear on the friezes at Borobhodur, Java, the largest architectural monument the Buddhist world has produced.

Āryaśūra did not simply retell the old stories though, setting them unaltered into elegant scholarly verse. It seems he was possessed by their spirit.

What is the Jātaka spirit? I don't know exactly, it is so ancient and stands in such contrast to the economic, political, and philosophical assumptions governing the contemporary world. There had been a goddess of forest and wilderness, Araṇyāṇī, to whom the poets of the *Ṛg Veda* (ca. 1700 BCE), poets legendary even in Āryaśūra's day, sang a mysterious hymn. She or one of her sort must have snared Āryaśūra. Beyond simply recasting the old stories or embellishing them with sophisticated poetic

craft, Āryaśūra invented and inserted in his poem several of his own—
"gathered from the air a live tradition" in Ezra Pound's memorable phrase.
This of course is something that makes any poet's work memorable.

It is an inability to similarly gather from the air of history a live tradition that has characterized so much Western scholarship of the past centuries when it approaches the legends and lore of Asia. This is doubly sad. It
demeans the vibrant traditions of so much of the planet, as well as closing
off access to a trove of art and lore that are the heritage of all human beings. Until very recent years, when the Western approach to South Asia has
not been one of outright condescension, it seems based on a profound mis-
trust. In London in 1920 the British Sanskrit scholar A.B. Keith published *A
History of Sanskrit Literature,* still considered the standard account of classical
India's literature. Summoning a common attitude towards the art of the
non-Western cultures Europe had colonized and pillaged (India a British
colony, the "jewel in the crown" of Empire, until 1949), Keith says of
Āryaśūra's Jātaka stories:

> Their chief defect to modern taste, is the extravagance which refuses
> to recognize the Aristotelian mean. The very first tale . . . tells of the
> . . . Bodhisattva who insists on sacrificing his life in order to feed a
> hungry tigress, whom he finds on the point of devouring the young
> whom she can no longer feed . . . the other narratives are no less inhu-
> man in the disproportion between the worth of the object sacrificed
> and that for whose sake the sacrifice is made. But these defects were
> deemed rather merits by contemporary . . . taste.

Nothing in Keith's experience, nothing in two thousand years of Occidental scholarship or metaphysics, had prepared him for an encounter with
this kind of poetry—which is to say this kind of thinking.

Bring the notion instantly up to date, and one can only wonder what
Professor Keith would have said of Mark Dubois, Earth First! activist who in
May 1979 chained himself to a boulder attempting to halt the damming of
California's Stanislaus River. Or what his attitude would have been towards
Ron Hoover, who in 1985 up in the Middle Santiam squatted on top of a tree
he dubbed Ygdrasil after the world-tree of Celtic myth, and refused to come

down, daring the timber company to fell it. What might he have said of Ron Watson, cheerful and irreverent Captain of the Sea Shepherds, who handcuffed himself to a pile of harbor seal pelts, was lifted by angry seal hunters with a ship's loading crane and dunked repeatedly in the Arctic Ocean until friends came to his rescue? I am citing only a few celebrated instances of North American activists here. One could augment the list of recent activists with citizens from every continent. What would Keith have said—what do dozens of contemporary moralists say today—of men, women and children across the planet who are risking their health, lives, bank accounts, and jobs in defense of forests, watersheds, valleys, endangered plant and animal species, traditional farmlands, and wild species habitat?

Buddhists believe we are all incipient Buddhas—the texts speak of a germ (*garbha*) of enlightenment within every sentient creature—migrating through incalculable reaches of time and space, navigating a complicated succession of births, each on course to ultimate Buddhahood. In other words, the stories of the Buddha's former births, heaped up by the hundreds, are not somebody else's story but one's own. They recount the births and deaths all creatures collectively come upon during the course of the voyage. What we have begun to witness in our own day among eco-activists—among indigenous resistance groups in India, Mexico, Brazil, and elsewhere; among radical animal rights workers; among any who draw the line against calculated, mechanized, profit-driven destruction of wild lands—is a resurgence of the old spirit of the *Jātaka Tales*. In our current period the spirit is made increasingly urgent, as well as vivid and elegant, by newly developed insights into ecology and biodiversity. Makers of story are everywhere being born around us, wakening the old spirit, adding like Āryaśūra did their own tales to the *Garland of Birth Stories*.

Did I say makers of story? In 1608 the Buddhist historian Tāranātha (his account survives in a Tibetan version) wrote the only known account of Āryaśūra's death. Tāranātha says Āryaśūra was traveling through a dense Himalayan glade when he encountered a starving tigress on the verge of devouring her own cubs. In one of those enchanted moments, the curtain between literature and life drawing utterly aside, Āryaśūra offered his own body to stem the tigress's famine. Tāranātha adds that before Āryaśūra died of his injuries he calmly set out seventy verses of poetry, written in his own blood. Unhappily, none of those verses are preserved in the books that come down to us. Maybe it does not matter. Who would be prepared to read them?

In India literary tradition maintains that the Sanskrit epic *Rāmāyaṇa* is the first poem. Its author, Vālmīki (date unknown), holds the title *adikavi*, "first poet." One might interpret the title to mean something like "most eminent." In the opening section of *Rāmāyaṇa* he gives a compelling just-so story, an account of the origin of his poem and thus of poetry. The story goes that one day, leaving the hermitage of his teacher, he had taken a stroll through the forest. It was springtime in India and Vālmīki was studying with delight the trees, the newly budded flowers, the high creeks, the colorful insects, the birds and animals. He pushed his way out to a clearing. As he stood in the brush at its edge he saw mating in the grass, a pair of *krauncha* birds—a type of curlew. The birds were utterly absorbed in their love play, and Vālmīki watched transfixed. Without warning, from the opposite side of the meadow, out of a blind stepped a hunter. He callously raised his bow, let fly an arrow, and with one terrible and accurate shot killed the male *krauncha*. The female bird cast herself in the dirt next to her fallen mate, released a miserable cry, and beat her wings in horror. Vālmīki, aghast at the scene, felt a spontaneous curse wrenched from his throat—

> Sportsman—
> for senselessly killing
> one of these
> passion-gripped *krauncha* birds
> you will never
> through the years of your life
> find a resting place!

Indian tradition holds this curse to be the first poem. Critics of course find Vālmīki's claim to have discovered poetry fabulous, a rather improbable beginning to India's output of poetry, which is massive and occurs in dozens of languages. But an important truth lurks here: the belief in India that *the world's first poetic stanza emerged in a fit of outrage over the wanton destruction of wildlife.*

Poetry to the people of India, whether it crystallizes a mood of compassion, romance, rage, humor, or tranquility, has some intimate, original connection with wildlife and wild lands—and with grief at their unjustified destruction. It is no accident that India has also been the place where Hindu and Buddhist thinkers have most experimentally advanced the concept of *ahiṃsā*, non-injury, or non-killing. (More realistically this has been put as no wanton killing or harming of any sentient creature.) Buddha made it a cornerstone of his teaching, and in the twentieth century the statesman and prophetic environmentalist Mahatma Gandhi founded his political strategies on it.

India is also the legendary and not-so-legendary terrain where cross-species empathy gets taken to extremes witnessed nowhere else on the planet. I think of two institutions in particular, the *goshala* and the *pindrajole*, both associated with the Jain religion and supported by donations from members of the community. A goshala is a hostel for the care of aged, infirm and sick bovines, sanctuaries where cattle no longer able to care for themselves, or which have become a burden to family or keeper, live out their lives, sheltered and fed with a modicum of dignity. These are very much old age homes for cattle. Lest anyone think this merely confirms the archaic Indo-European mystique with cattle, still highly visible in India, I mention the pindrajole, an institution which extends sympathy to all manner of animal, domestic and wild. Several pindrajoles in India specialize in caring for insects.

There are those who regard the taking of any animal life, wild or other, as unjustified. There are some who extend their notion of cross-species kinship to compass, not mammals or birds or fish in isolation, but the larger systems within which individual creatures emerge and vanish in the metabolic weavings of evolution. These systems include forests, rivers, watersheds, mountain ranges, oceans and cities. I said the appearance in recent years of eco-activists across the planet is a resurgence of an ancient contract of kinship. I would like now to formally name that old understanding *jātaka mind*.

Activist movements that exemplify this kind of thought have been emerging in recent decades in India; maybe resurging is a better word. One that has received the most international attention has been the Chipko movement, which within environmental circles has achieved legendary status. By legendary I don't mean to imply something fabulous; I mean that stories of Chipko's activities sustain and inspire eco-activists both inside India and beyond her borders.

The Chipko movement represents the confluence of three streams. There is the old spirit of the *Jātaka Tales*, ever ready to erupt into the folklife of the Indian people. There is the development of contemporary scientific understanding of ecosystems and how they operate. And there is the blend of civil disobedience, non-violence, and on-the-table activism which Mahatma Gandhi, having read Thoreau's essay *On Civil Disobedience,* pioneered in the first half of the twentieth century.

Thousands of years before Gandhi walked the planet there had been in India a tradition of *Realpolitik* laid forth in old treatises. This tradition, still hanging on after Gandhi's death both in India and in practically every other nation state, enumerates four time-honored methods of achieving political ends: sowing dissent, negotiation, bribery, and open assault. The Chipko movement had other ideas though. "Let your actions set the finer points of your philosophy," says founding member of Earth First! Dave Forman, and in keeping with that adage, rather than treating Gandhian environmental activism as a theoretical system, I will try to illustrate the spirit of the Chipko activists. This is proper I think, because Chipko has a thoroughly improvisational character: not ritual but experiment, not dogma but story.

Chipko emerged in the Garhwal Himalaya, foothills of the high northern mountains, where in modern times the finest and most extensive forests of India have grown. India: a continent of almost a billion people with an enormous appetite for wood: for fuel, for fodder, for timber. Almost all this wood has had to come out of the forested Himalayan foothills. The mountain slopes have as a result suffered severe deforestation over the last couple of centuries, leading to the washing away of topsoils, flooding of the plains below, destruction of farmland, wreckage of village and grove by flood and landslide, death of people and livestock; ultimately, the progressive degradation of much of northern India.

One principal problem with the mountain regions was that in the 1960s India and China fought a war over disputed boundary lines. The best

way any government has found to stabilize uncertain borderlands is to rap-
idly develop the area, a course the government of New Delhi pursued. For
the forests of the Himalayan foothills, development tipped an already precarious situation. In the late sixties, as the connection between rapid population growth, clearcut timber policies, and decline of the region's ecological vitality became clear, a number of activists began to speak up in the Himalayan regions, using traditional mountain methods to activate support
for a decentralized forest management. They called village assemblies; they
went on *padayātrā*, or pilgrimage by foot, from village to village; they per-
formed folksong, theatre and dance, dramatizing the connection between
large scale development and collapsing village economies.

In March of 1973 the Simon Company, located in the industrial city of
Allahabad, Uttar Pradesh, was given a contract to harvest a forest of ash
trees in the Garhwal. Timber companies had been receiving regular government contracts, but the Simon Company's seemed particularly egre-
gious—the company specialized in sporting goods. Ash wood is used in the
United States for baseball bats, in India for cricket bats. I think there is a
direct if unarticulated connection here, which loops back to Vālmīki's outrage at seeing a hunter kill a bird in sport. Local activists, setting their
jaws, gathered in the village that had traditionally possessed rights to the
trees of this forest, and tried to figure out what they could do to stop the
clearcutting of their only material resource. Nobody knows how the term
first cropped up, one story has an elderly blind folksinger coining it—
chipko is a Hindi word that means hug—but by meeting's end the villagers
had resolved to go out and hug their trees, putting their bodies between
tree and the cutters' equipment.

Similar protests in the past had met with terrific violence, particularly
in isolated regions. But this time, against everyone's expectations, the strat-
egy worked. The Simon Company and its government lobbyists backed
down in the face of widespread publicity.

The following year at the village of Reni, another forest was given out
on contract. Many of the local residents were tribal people who had lost
long-held territories during the war with China. When the Indian government and corporate timber interests discovered that activists planned a
tree-hugging campaign at Reni, they utilized some of the age-old political

expedients: bribery, negotiation, and sowing dissent. First of all, they informed the regional organizer of Chipko, Chandi Prasad Bhatt, that they were ready to include him in forest management policy, and so drew him off to a distant town. They then announced to the men of Reni village that monetary reimbursement for lands lost during the China-India war would be handed out at another village. All the men, expectably, set out for the journey. And an army of timber cutters slipped in, in buses with shuttered windows. One village girl happened to be out gathering fodder, and saw the buses unload. She rushed back to the village and told Gaura Devi, local woman of greatest authority, what she had seen.

Gaura Devi quickly rounded up the village women, and they thronged into the forest ahead of the slow-moving lumberjacks. The tree cutters, many of whom were drinking, arrived with their axes and found a cluster of women confronting them. They did not know what to make of the situation, but a foreman drunkenly pulled a gun and pointed it at the protesters. Gaura Devi stepped forward, opening her bosom, and reputedly said, "The forest is like our Mother. Shoot me instead." At this the workers fell apart in shame and confusion. They left their tools, turned around, and began picking their way back along the forest path. The women followed, retrieving the discarded tools and using them to dislodge a concrete walkway that gave passage over an avalanche ravine, cutting off access to the forest. They saved their trees.

There are loops and cycles of story that move without the constraints of chronology. One loop brings medieval Rajasthan into the garland. It was there that in 1485 the son of a village headman had a vision in which he saw ahead for his people a period of terrific hardship caused by callous human disregard for nature. He founded a small sect called the Bishnoi, and laid down twenty-nine tenets which Bishnoi observe to this day. Foremost among the tenets were a prohibition on the cutting of green wood, a prohibition on cremation (which requires prodigious amounts of timber—he instituted burial instead), and a ban on the killing of wild animals. The growth of trees and the flourishing of wildlife in Bishnoi areas caused their village lands to become green, prosperous, good for farmland, good for cattle, while the rest of Rajasthan, lacking governance over a burgeoning population, was suffering desertification.

In 1731 a nearby Maharaja decided to build himself a palace. Needing wood to fuel his lime kilns he sent men to Jalnadi village, about ten miles from present day Jodhpur, to collect wood. When the axe carriers showed up to cut Bishnoi forest, a woman named Amrita Devi confronted them. She implored them not to cut the trees, but meeting with no sympathy declared the cutters' axes would have to go through her to reach the trees. She hugged a tree, and as the woodsmen's axes fell gave out a cry which became a Bishnoi slogan: "A chopped head costs less than a felled tree."

As Amrita Devi's body fell into pieces, each of her three daughters immediately and in succession replaced her. After this harrowing incident, the woodsmen retreated for reinforcements, while the local Bishnoi sent out a call to their neighboring villages, eighty-four in all. Of those eighty-four villages, all sent support save a single one which to its eternal shame did not respond. The woodsmen returned to continue their tree-felling, and by day's end had killed another three hundred fifty-nine people. Altogether two hundred ninety-four men and sixty-nine women died. Moreover the cutters had secured only a third of the timber they'd been charged to collect. When the Maharaja discovered their failure he was livid and hurried to the site to assign responsibility. But seeing the scattered, mutilated bodies, he underwent an instant change of heart and put a blanket ban on tree-cutting in Bishnoi areas.

Today a shrine stands where Amrita Devi fell.

So we arrive at a point of bewildering excess. What can one do except draw back and acknowledge the emergence of something unnamable? Something that overwhelms a merely economic, or anthropocentric concern for the environment? An utterly mysterious sensibility, underlying the ecological webwork, has declared itself. "The forest is like our Mother," insisted Gaura Devi. Mahāyāna Buddhism similarly charges the practitioner to regard every creature possessing a nervous system, however rudimentary, as motherlike. The *Prajñā-pāramitā* texts, which include the *Diamond* and *Heart* sūtras speak repeatedly of "motherlike sentient beings." In the beginningless round of birth and rebirth that all are subject to—says an intricate series of commentaries—in the perennially growing garland of *Jātakas*, every incarnate creature has at some point been one's own mother.

Every living creature should thus be treated with an according respect. This vision, urgent in today's world as it is tender, is also an expression of how lonely we will feel as human beings when a day dawns without spotted owls, with no ivory-tusked mammals, no marbled murrelets, no whales, no clean beaches, no moss-draped old growth redwoods.

So close to our probable future, this loneliness—and many have begun to suffer it grievously—is a stirring of jātaka mind.

A moment ago I touched on India's tradition of Realpolitik, which advocates four calculated responses to crisis, four strategies calibrated to the immediate demands of the State. Beyond these conventional methods a confounding array of non-cynical, non-selfserving responses manage to persist. They spring from deeper emotional sources, sources that no short-term consideration of personal benefit can conceal. One delicate instance occurred in a poem from ancient Maharashtra State. It is an anonymous poem, about two thousand years old.

> Lone buck
> in the clearing
> nearby doe
> eyes him with such
> longing
> that there
> in the trees the hunter
> seeing his own girl
> lets the bow drop
>   —ca. 200, from King Hāla's *Gāhākoṣa*

Something fresh and shy, something with a profound and unpredictable intelligence has revealed itself. That intelligence is growing bolder right now. Worldwide environmental degradation has drawn forth countless responses, non-cynical and non-compromising. India, Brazil, Indonesia, California. There's protest over the clear-cutting of forests, over the damming of rivers, over the strip-mining of mountains, over poaching and "licensed" (state-sanctioned poaching) of endangered animal species. Will popular movements and the slow work of legislation prove adequate to protect billions of years of coevolution from a seemingly unstoppable global economy?

In this country, one manifestation of that intelligence has been nearly endemic since the nineteen-seventies. Though the mainstream press, in the hands of a few recently empowered megacorporations, depict it as aberrant and criminal, actions known as *monkeywrenching* take place with gathering urgency. An old term, monkey wrench, origins unknown says my *American Heritage Dictionary*. It was playfully introduced as both adjective and verb to current eco-language by Edward Abbey in his lively novel *The Monkeywrench Gang*. Informal jargon, but let me hazard a definition: *preemptive acts that disable the machinery of destruction*.

Such as it occurs, monkeywrenching does not seem to get carried out by organized groups. It looks more like the scattered response of an escalating number of *homo sapiens* in many countries to illegal or outrageous assaults on ecological integrity. Forget the sensational press. Monkeywrenchers adhere to tenets of non-injury. This is important: despite how eco-activists are depicted in the newspapers and on the nightly news (even by timid environmental lobby groups), monkeywrenching is not terrorism. Its proponents and their samizdat instruction manuals make clear that all maneuvers are calculated to avoid human injury. Outside-the-law activists have made their statements without ambiguity, though: they will no longer tolerate the sacrifice of wildlife and wild lands, nor the biological viability of this planet, to the imperatives of Capitalist profit, or to Socialist mythologies of industrial progress.

Hugging trees, dismantling bulldozers, "liberating" laboratory animals, sitting in trees and defying the timber corporations, chasing endangered game species away from the hunter's gun, clipping fences erected by private interests on public land, barricading illegal dirt bike trails. In these and similar acts of resistance one can see emerging among planetary eco-activists the same mind that told itself through the *Jātaka Tales*.

Across the many political and ecological zones of the world (India and North America for instance) profound social differences exist. Acts of cross-species empathy or the defense of wild lands, being improvisational and in response to daily outrages, take a variety of forms. New responses are sure to emerge in the future. But jātaka mind no more restricts itself to a single culture than do the acts that provoke it: environmental degradation, corporate wangling, or simple human cruelty.

Once the Buddha was born an ibex with splendid ebony horns that swept gracefully back over his head. He wandered like a hermit deep in an unvisited forest, drinking pure water, feeding on greenery, and roaming as he pleased. One bright day the king of a nearby domain decided to hunt in this forest and brought a noisy entourage along. So excited by the chase was the king that once in the woods he romped ahead on his best steed, leaving his soldiers and horses behind.

He pursued creature after creature with his bow, shooting down deer, rabbit, antelope, and numerous bird species with unerring accuracy, leaving a litter of carcasses for his men to retrieve. Entering a quiet glade he spotted the ibex with its unmistakable set of horns, and thrilling to the chase spurred his horse. The ibex fled towards a precipitous ravine, leaped in an unbroken motion across its rim, and continued to run. But a moment later it no longer heard pursuing hooves. Curious, the ibex drew to a halt, and craned his neck backwards. There at the edge of the ravine, pacing nervously, was a riderless steed.

"The hunter must have been high in his stirrups, hands drawing his bow, and unable to grip his reins when his horse balked at the edge," thought the ibex. "He has been tossed down." The thought of an injured man filled his mind with distress and his heart with sympathy. He bounded back to the ravine. Looking down he saw the king lying in the gully twenty feet below. The king's armor had protected him from mortal injury, but he was badly shaken and unable to climb the steep cliff sides. "I am not a demon but a resident of this forest," called the ibex. "I can carry you out if you'll trust me." And he dropped with agility down the side of the gorge, springing from ledge to ledge. At the bottom he bowed and offered his back to the dazed king, who mounted him like a horse. In a few moments the ibex had reunited the king with his charger.

"How can I reward you?" asked the king, shamed that a few moments before he had treated this dignified creature like an object of sport. "You will come with me to my palace. You can live there in comfort and safety. Life in the forest must be harsh —large cats in the brush, human hunters running you down, food and shelter unreliable at best, hot weather and cold, tormenting insects all year long. I will house you in my palace yards."

"The forest is my home," replied the ibex. "If you think I would enjoy life in a palace you are gravely mistaken. Humans find one habitat suits them, but the forest suits the wild animal. Without my solitude, unable to roam the meadows freely, my life would be miserable." Looking at the humbled king the ibex added, "If you would like to reward me then grant me a favor—give up hunting for sport. All creatures are alike in their affections, their fears, their pleasures and pain. Why should you do to another animal what done to you would bring panic, injury, and violent death?" The king lowered his head.

Turning, the ibex trotted into a thicket of greenery. In a moment it had vanished from sight.

Avalokiteśvara, Rocky Flats,
& *The New York Times*

Edited from a conference sponsored by the Academy of American Poets and held at Poet's House in New York City on October 28, 1992, to discuss ideas raised by the anthology Beneath a Single Moon: Buddhism and Contemporary American Poetry *(Shambhala Publications, 1991).*

The Place

IT IS A PRIVILEGE to be here, present at the beginning of a magnificent project, probably a 1000 year project at least: the naturalization of Buddhist thought and practice to the American landscape. Despite Buddhist populations entering this country with Chinese immigrants as early as the 1870s, they seem sufficiently new to this continent that most of the population looks on Buddhism as an exotic transplant. Several distinct schools have taken hold over the past century, adapting themselves to their new surroundings. This suggests that ours may be the first generation on the North American continent to find itself pondering forms of practice distinct to our own culture, in the way China, Tibet, Japan, Burma and Thailand devised forms no longer reliant on the traditions of India.

Sometimes, considering the many dedicated practice centers stretching from New York to San Francisco (the first two North American cities to house Buddhist centers), I think Buddhism is about to settle in decisively. Yet just when it looks like something durable has been accomplished, a sobering corrective arrives if I touch in with Philip Whalen at his Hartford Street Zen Center residence. Philip treats Buddhist practice like a tender little shoot: it needs to be watered and carefully attended every day or its shallow root system may wither with disheartening speed.

If the histories of China or Tibet set a precedence, Buddhist practice will take many generations to find its unique shapes here, suited to our particular North American bioregions and unique mix of peoples. It has taken most of the current residents—children and grandchildren of people who came out of Europe, Asia or Africa—generations to settle down with some degree of familiarity on this landmass. We still haven't as a nation developed durable skills for long term neighborhood design or given rise to a generous sense of comradeship among white, African, Hispanic, Asian, and Native people.

I recently moved to Colorado from seventeen years on the West Coast. My new residence lies on the eastern edge of the spine of our continent, where the jagged Front Range of the Rocky Mountains lifts abruptly off the shortgrass prairies. Slowly I'm learning to recognize who else lives in this region, right at the shifting piedmont where the Great Plains, gradually shelving upwards from the Mississippi, cut into ponderosa pine forest. Higher come the aspen groves, then mixed fir and spruce, delicate tundra with funny-shaped dwarf trees that have sculpted themselves to withstand high altitude winds. Finally comes the last pitch, into rugged high rock of Indian Peaks Wilderness and the Continental Divide. Ten thousand years ago the mountains were heavily glaciated. Today they are an immediate attraction to walk into, even in winter. There goes a common raven, wheeling across high remote cliffs. Pika's sharp whistle below in the rocks.

For millennia these mountains were non-residential zones for trade and summer hunting; the way in was by foot. It still is, particularly if you want to get intimate with the non-human residents of alpine or tundra ecozones. Down below lie the grasslands, threaded with their own irresistible flora and fauna. To explore these I do what Indo-European ancestors have done for centuries on steppeland and prairie, which is go out on horseback. Often I take my five year old daughter, Althea, and a couple of seasoned roans. Rambling the plains we can glance west into the snowcaps, but the noticeable local creatures are swift fox, black-tail prairie dog, cottontail, bullsnake. Upwards circle ferruginous hawks; if we're lucky an eagle or peregrine falcon. A whole webwork of flora I've never encountered before leaves burrs on the horse flanks; blue gramma's the native grass underfoot, common lupine down in the washes. Where prairie dog towns and anthills and human disturbances toss up the soil, plant opportunists with tough pioneer names have come in—cheatgrass, ragweed, and the viciously imperialist spotted knapweed.

To look at yourself then not as a lone person riding through, casting the solitary shadow of old Westerns, but as a knot of metabolism in the intricate webbing: grasses and forbes, angiosperms that fed herds of large mammals. Looking close to the trail you see ground squirrel teeth and twisted hair where a coyote shat. Into this non-human realm is tucked the venerable art of domestication (a Neolithic science, it's original strategies long lost): a mystery how the horse responds to a human child's hand on the reins.

As we drop into gullies, then ride up onto lowlying mesas where the horses can really stretch out, we have an uninterrupted view south and west to a fenced compound of three hundred and sixty acres. This is the industrial core of Rocky Flats, former plutonium trigger factory, which began production in 1953, the year I was born. Its buildings and lots are known by identifying numbers, some of them locally infamous. There's Building 707 where plutonium triggers were manufactured; there's the 903 Pad Area where thousands of drums filled with contaminated cutting oil leaked in the 1960s and high wind carried the contaminated topsoil sixteen miles into downtown Denver. Building 776-777 caught fire in 1969, the largest and costliest industrial fire in history though flames never breached the outer walls. Rocky Flats stores in its buildings 14.2 metric tons of plutonium and nearly eight tons of weapons grade Uranium, manufactured from 1953 until 1989 when a joint raid by the FBI and EPA closed down production for flagrant violation of environmental and safety laws. These figures do not account for significant residues trapped in the 4.6 miles of ductwork.

Plutonium, manufactured for only one purpose, the develement of weapons of mass destruction. Obsolete within decades of its invention. Stored in makeshift 1950s shacks built to last twenty-five years. Nobody knows what to do with the plutonium, stored in those dilapidated buff-colored buildings just past the barbed wire. It will remain toxic long past the next glaciation. I look back at my daughter urging her horse on and wonder what kind of world she is growing up into.

The Times

Walking the streets of Manhattan recently, a friend quoted me something she'd heard: a person who reads the Sunday *New York Times* gets more information in one sitting than any human received a hundred years ago in a lifetime. That stopped me in my tracks. There was something terribly wrong. As though the ordinary business of the newspaper—stirring up hunger for pointless luxuries, or issuing reports on capitalist intrigues here and abroad—are information far beyond the precise science and art humans have practiced during their duration on earth.

Information is not simply raw data, measured in bulk, set out to trouble the already turgid human mind. Information I'd argue is intelligible design, structure that makes sense. Stuff you can work with. "Patterned energy" might be a good term. The more intelligible the pattern, the more precise the information. If a mass of subject matter does not have a pattern to it, if a well-read adult can only respond to most of it with confusion, anguish, disinterest or helplessness, maybe better to simply call it "noise."

That leaves the question, how do you respond to the noise? Noise of the infinitely forgettable sports page or stock market report? Noise of the book reviews, food columns, editorials, advertisements? The noise of contaminated beakers at Rocky Flats, rattling for no known reason just a few hundred yards from fieldmouse and goat and human babies? Whether you believe what the *Times* says, or like the leftist press regard it as mostly evasion and disinformation doesn't much matter. That cacophonous noise, listened to in a different spirit, carries something profound. Could it be the wrenching cries of misery, which rise every day across our planet? The sound Avalokiteśvara heard millennia back?

The Handful of Seeds

Avalokiteśvara was a north Indian prince of the 5th century BCE who became a brilliant and disciplined student of Shakyamuni Buddha. Old texts say he pursued his discipline so singlemindedly that in his own lifetime he came to the threshold of enlightenment, and was about to cross into Nirvana, free of the webs of biological and political interdependence which include hunting, eating, killing, buying & selling, and the range of human avarice. But at the last moment he heard a terrible noise rising behind him. Pausing, he looked back over his shoulder—the texts say "downwards," and this gives him his Sanskrit name, Avalokiteśvara, "the lord who looks downwards." He saw that the clamor behind him was the aggregate cry of suffering creatures, lifting from countless world systems. He made a vow on the spot: not to enter Nirvana and extinguish his own griefs until he had freed each sentient creature from misery. As the Tibetans tenderly say, freed them down to the last blade of grass.

Acknowledgment of that cry—confusion, anguish, complexity, fragile doomed beauty, toxic mistake—is where Buddhism and poetry perhaps twine together. Both occur as efforts to hear the world's noise, the noise of sentient beings in their mixed pain and delight, however discordant—to discern an order, a pattern, in hopes of easing the misery.

The account of Avalokiteśvara's vow is central to Mahāyāna Buddhism, an unbroken 2500 year experiment. Experiment, I say, because Buddhist thought has been a mutable, cosmopolitan tradition, one based on innovations of the sort the human sapient brain is so clever at. An experimental performance that adapts itself from culture to culture, language to language, as sequential generations order the "noise" that surrounds them, and pass on what they've learnt. In terms of structuring one's world, locating a pattern by which to order the evidence of your human perceptions and sharp mind, there is a good deal more information in something like a sonnet, a blues lyric, or a haiku, than in the Sunday *Time's* wasteful, insistent advertising insert. A poem or a song may seem little patterns, but they stay with us.

Ethnobotanist Gary Paul Nabhan writes, "In a handful of wild seeds taken from any one natural community, there is hidden the distillation of millions of years of coevolution of plants and animals." Looking down into this handful—and it seems to be a specific handful of seeds he is speaking of—he observes that it holds, "more information than is contained in the Library of Congress." Clearly he is using the word information in a very deliberate sense.

Why have several dozen haiku by Bashō, Issa and Buson outlasted every news report issued by the *New York Times*? Why do the writings of Shakespeare and Jane Austen continue to spur serious talk? Cut-up poems

I've seen students do from newspapers have more durable interest than the news reports they came from—more humor, more warmth. Highly ordered verbal patterns—a good joke, a memorable jump-rope rhyme—something like poetry—must be consistently useful and pleasurable or they would not remain, passed on by children at recess. That's why Zen schools use sharp little baffling poems to develop the mind, and Tibetan anchorites frame their meditations in ballad form.

Consider the information an early twentieth century Bantu poet passed along. From Jermome Rothenberg's *Technicians of the Sacred* I take two lines which stand on their own as a discrete verse or haiku-like juxtaposition of images. You feel you might almost know the man, so much complexity has he patterned into his words:

> *The sound of a cracked elephant tusk.*
> *The anger of a hungry man.*
> (Jerome Rothenberg, *Technicians of the Sacred*)

Or from the *Zenrin Kushu*, a saying Zen students have cut their teeth on for centuries—

> *An itchy dog doesn't want*
> *rebirth in heaven,*
> *He sneers at white*
> *cranes in the clouds.*

William Everson Recollections

SOMEBODY HAD SAID, "I can't take anyone seriously who dresses like Davy Crockett." With Whitmanesque hair and beard though, a stained leather vest, wide-brimmed Western hat, outdoor boots, and a conspicuous bearclaw necklace at his throat, Bill Everson more resembled Joaquin Miller who led a Modoc fighting force against white settlers, or even "hawk-hearted" bandit Murietta whose pickled head sat in a jar on the sheriff's desk in Bill's early poem from *The Residual Years*.

Everson taught a class at the University of California, Santa Cruz, in a huge makeshift Buckminster Fuller dome of warped plywood and protruding nails, set out in a parking lot. The class had a reputation as sort of a local spectacle, because Bill would stand and brood, meditate and thunder for a couple of hours a week in the center of the dome and no one was permitted to interrupt. I looked in once and saw the students lying about derelict, asleep or stretched into a yoga position or doodling in notebooks, and never went back. At poetry readings it was different; I felt instantly attracted to that blue eye full of humorous sparks. The crashing drama of his poetry. The thunderous self-dramatization that paradoxically seemed without guile. That's how you want to get old, I thought.

It was when I got interested in book arts and printing that I went looking for Bill. At the invitation of Rita Bottoms, Special Collections librarian at U.C. Santa Cruz, Bill had arrived and established the Lime Kiln Press in a lower room of the library. The press might have been named for Robinson Jeffers' poem "Bixby Landing." More likely it memorialized the abandoned nineteenth century lime kilns that litter the redwood forests around Santa Cruz—crumbling pits and outsize towers of mortared stone, they could have been ancient castle keeps, older and more blasted than any Rhone Valley rampart from Eleanor of Aquitaine's time. Strange that these deserted furnaces of California only date back a hundred years. Several notable ones lie scattered through the Santa Cruz campus forests and are popular refuges to which young lovers slip off.

It was early Spring of 1978. I asked Bill if I could work with him on one of Lime Kiln's printing projects. Letterpress printing interested me as a way of turning my affection for books into an impractical but gratifying craft; I had slowly begun to arrive at a sense of myself as a poet. Here was a man who pursued both arts.

The Lime Kiln Press, operating under the auspices of the University, was a regular accredited college course and Bill's assistants and printer's devils in those years were enrolled students. My request was not improper, just irregular since I was not a student. Maybe it was my enthusiasm for Ananda Coomaraswamy's writings, books which had been important to Bill, or maybe he hoped to have someone who could talk with him about the obscure Essex House Press and the type fonts of Eric Gill. He invited me to come around and work with his small group of apprentices. When I joined them, the group had already designed and partly printed the current book—an edition of Bill's poem "Blame It on the Jet Stream," which he'd declaimed at graduation for the University's Kresge College a year or two earlier. "Jet Stream" is a wild poem, very much Jeffers in spirit. It gets at both the furious coastal California weather patterns of the jet-stream years, which brought fantastic rain storms into the redwood forests, and the equally notable violence that stunned Santa Cruz in the early 1970s. On the model of Gilroy the "garlic capital" and Castroville the "artichoke capital," locals had taken to calling Santa Cruz the "mass murder capital of the world." Underneath its counterculture veneer a lot of killing had gone down. One troubled killer had preyed on women students from the campus.

It's a tough poem, "Blame it on the Jet Stream," with long prophetic lines—Whitman in cadence, slightly Biblical in its anger, but all Jeffers in how it pins a steady cold eye on violence and sacrament. Now Bill was seeing it through the demanding craftwork that would make it a book in the slow old tradition of the arts and crafts movements. Not so ambitious or risky a project as *Granite & Cypress*, the Jeffers book Bill had printed at Lime Kiln, and which had restored his reputation after a long absence from printing. But that book, bound into an enormous standing case of

Monterey cypress inset with a panel of granite from Jeffers' own quarry, had been a tribute to the one poet Bill called master.

We worked the Acorn handpress, same design, nearly the same device as the old Washington Bill had bought when he'd first drifted down the coast to Berkeley after doing his wartime internment in a conscientious objector's camp at Walport, Oregon. That press had helped found the Bay Area poetry renaissance.

> . . . once it is made ready, the right impression achieved, and the bearing-off points placed on the bed; once printing is begun and the run fairly under way, it moves into the work with a wonderful dispatch, its very spareness stands it in stead; and so perfectly gauged are its meeting parts that I do not see how, impression for impression, any handpress could do better.

At Lime Kiln we labored the thick ink. I'd never seen such stuff, digging it from a battered tin with a gleaming steel spatula, hammering it with a wooden mallet till it was pliant enough to cover the hand-held rubber roller, laying it across the bed of Goudy Modern type. We lifted the dampened paper, fed sheets into the frisket. Everyone levered the great horizontal handle of polished wood which screwed down the press to achieve an impression. In words it sounds easy, but it took months of painstaking labor, checking our handiwork at every click of the press. People were in good humor, particularly Bill who kept embellishing with new instalments the account of how Susanna, his wife, had kicked him out of their shack at Kingfisher Flat. I think by this time he'd moved back in. He recounted the story with amusement, swaggering and cocky, so you could feel the pain he was trying to conceal underneath. He was sixty-six years old. A young Cherokee woman—Bill said she was twenty-eight—had something to do with it. She used to sit with him at poetry readings in the local cafes. I bet she was the last woman: the last before he began to dramatically & publicly suffer first an onset of impotence, then Parkinson's disease—anguished days memorialized in *Masks of Drought*.

We finished the print run of *Jet Stream*. Pages with their sharp blue & black print; the woodcut of Bill as a frontispiece; the hidden watermark— "Veronica's napkin" he showed me. His eye moist when he held a page up to the window to backlight the watermark, so I knew it was sexiness more than piety in the womanly Christ image that drew him. Though he adored the paper itself. That was what mattered when you got down to craft, how its fibers expanded & took the swift keen bite of lead and ink.

The semester ran out at school and the students drifted away. Working alone with him over the summer weeks I noticed his eyes were giving him trouble and the first discernible tremblings of Parkinson's had set in. I'd watched him occasionally lift a printed sheet to the light while others had fed the press, screwing his whiskers and eyeglasses up to question how the ink had taken, occasionally insisting on reworking some page. Nothing seemed wrong at the time. Thinking back, I believe it was hard to see well in that enclosed lower room, despite the overhead lights.

We met upstairs in the Special Collections library to collate the sheets one day. A big airy room with long gleaming oak tables; through large windows sunlight was slanting through the redwoods and reddish amber particles of redwood fiber drifted into the room. Excellent light to judge the quality of the printing.

. . . with the handpress, more than any other device, everything resolves back to the self.

We laid the pages out on tables in sequential order and started to collect them into books. The two or three librarians kept a quiet distance, working their own job, but the room rippled with tension. Another of Bill's exacting books was nearly ready to go to the binder. Bill hardly said a word to anyone. On the walls ten of Kenneth Patchen's picture poems looked down—bold, funny, unrestrained. Dashed off with humor and bold spontaneity. Cartoonlike. Probably the antithesis of the impossibly perfected book art Bill hankered after, had spent his life tracking through history. Broadsides and posters and single pages of poetry to him were simply ephemera. "Our keepsake mad country," he once wrote. Bill was in thrall of the Book. He called it an archetype, both in love and afraid of the grip it had on him. That's why he wanted to build books, from first page to last.

I heard a startling animal moan. I thought he was sick. Bill's hands were shaking uncontrollably, worse than I'd seen them. Parkinson's has a key emotional element, he once told me. Self-consciousness, embarrassment or anguish often brought him to an access of shaking. He even used it as a bit of a joke when he started a poetry reading. Now, a dried sheet of *Jet Stream* was rattling violently in his hands. It sounded like jet-stream wind in the leathery California live oaks leaves of the hills. His face was pale, horrified, inaccessible. Then, not suddenly, but as though it had been years in the making, a cry dragged up out of him—drawn from some dreadfully deep place—

"Forgive me!"

A low keening, each syllable painfully prolonged, an old man's howl. It might not have even been loud. But it was dreadful, incongruous, raw; and it came out again. "Forgive me!" I studied him, sideways, and kept to my sorting. Pages clearly off-register, with any stray glancing of ink, or muddied rather than bitten by type, these I set aside. A few unfortunate thumbprints. And all day as we gathered up sheets he would draw a page close to his face, nearly knocking his glasses off, his hands shook so fearsomely. Craft secrets lay there—intricacies of fiber expanded by moisture and cut by lead type-edges. Ink quality, the exacting process of pounding & laying on ink. The build-up of the platen, the register of the thing. My eyes could not even begin to detect the centuries of tradition he was looking for. What he was seeing defeated him though. That keening kept coming, so bitter, like the poem he had written, which was now totally subsumed in the printer's art.

For, with the handpress, more than any other printing device, everything resolves back to the self. When the results are spotty, almost certainly it is one's own fault—rarely the press's. Somewhere you erred...

I saw how much for him they were devotions—both the poetry and the printing, devotions—devotions to a God he'd spent his whole life struggling with. Raging against. Simpering up to. How he'd run just as much from as towards that God. How a failure in his craft didn't just mean a piece of botched work, something to rectify another day when the light was better or the air's moisture better adjusted. It implicated his life, his strength, his devotion. Sitting there in his hide & claw & bead clothing he looked primal and pagan. All that wild unpredictability people travel distant dangerous places just to catch a whiff of—all of it there, crouching in him, like in some lair. Rattling in his hands sheet after sheet of that poem with its high diction and evocation of violence and wildness. "Forgive me." His eye taking note of no poetry. Only the printer's errancy.

This coast, like all beautiful places, crying out for tragedy.

I guess I learnt more of religion that harrowing day than any book ever told me. Hour after hour punctuated by Bill's inalterable "Forgive me." He was too wild for piety. Bill gauged himself by a God I cannot understand. Years of thinking about it has not given me much of a glimpse. His was a God I could certainly never bow down to. In the last twenty years I've repeatedly had to listen to poets and critics dismiss Bill for what they call his self-dramatization. Let them. That intimate frightful irrepressibly wild behavior—all the defeat and dread and self-mortification driving his voice—was not just some head trip. It spoke to something "out there." *Out there.* Past the critics. Past books. Maybe past understanding. So far out there that even praying can't touch it.

Part of the terror of it, too, is that whatever you write and have published you can never escape; it follows you everywhere you live. That is also the problem of the printer: every book that he has spoiled by putting his hand to it will also hound him down through the ages.

Bill had a hellhound on his trail. That's why the books are so good.

We're in the crowded little clapboard outbuilding underneath the redwoods at Kingfisher Flat. It's the building Bill uses for his study. Several miles back from the coast. My faded blue Pontiac lines up alongside his Landrover in the clearing ringed by *Sequoia sempervirens,* the towering cathedral redwoods. Behind his cabin the creek winds through the forests, down to the jagged Homeric shoreline at Davenport where nineteenth century whalers set out to strike the Gray Whales migrating our coast. Here, a couple of miles inland, the cabin is crammed with books and papers—a massive table is stacked in disorder with printed matter, books & letters; file cabinets are overflowing; closet doors forced back by cartons. He has been rummaging for his manuscript *American Bard*.

As he looks for the elusive pages, Bill keeps uncovering mementos of his printer's craft and pulling them out to show me. Old woodblock prints, rare broadsides, drawers full of proofsheets and discards. Books from well-known presses, and presses I've never heard of. Back in an unreachable corner his Washington handpress. "Our keepsake mad country." Only the book interests him. I push him a bit—recounting something I read about the Bible in a special collections library in Houston which some pioneer bound in Indian skin. If Bill ever gets pious it's about archetypes, and the Book is a key one for him. He gives me a long look, then digs for something else.

It's the legendary printer's dream he worked on in 1953 when he had his Washington press working—*Novum Psalterium PII XII*. During his tenure at St. Albert's Priory in Oakland he had solicited and received permission to work on a psalter. He had to get permission because this was irregular work for a Dominican monk who was training for priesthood. To begin the project he had to discontinue his other studies. Many regard his psalter as the finest piece of craft printing ever achieved on this continent. Maybe the finest piece of craft printing *abandoned* is the right way to tell it. He's discussed the book in essays and interviews and his autobiographical writings. Look it up if you want. After he left off the project, about halfway printed, a wealthy collector got hold of his exquisite pages, had a commercial printer finish the rest of the pages, and had the thing bound. It's a hybrid, a strange mongrel of a book, half of it like they say, the finest print job done on our continent; the other half some job-printer's efforts to make a second half look like the first, with a completely different technology. There are only sixty-four copies. On the colophon page his copy says number two. Evidently some copies had ended up in his hands.

"I had number One sent to the Pope," he says. "Number Two I kept for myself. Number Three went to Cardinal Spellman. Sometimes people say, well Bill, where do you stand with the Church these days? I tell them the Pope received the first *Psalterium.* Number two came to me. Spellman got number three. That's where I stand."

His blue eye moist with amusement in that cascade of white hair.

A couple of years later, after I'd more or less lost contact with Bill Everson, I chanced to be back in Santa Cruz when Robert Bly came through town to give a reading. It was at that big modern church up off of High Street, and the hall held several hundred people. The audience was milling about getting settled when I arrived—a lot of folk in from the hills. I took a seat somewhere in the center of the auditorium. Bly was there early, up front speaking with friends and greeting his audience. At some point I glanced back and saw Bill arrive, stooped by his Parkinson's, clutching a cane. He looked old as granite but shifted his way down the aisle with dignity and restraint. A young friend had him by the arm. They found some seats ten rows from the stage, had to climb past a number of people to get there, and it was a struggle for Bill to get in at all. I thought I'd wait to speak to him until he was settled—it took all his concentration to get that troubled, awkward, shaking old body down an aisle, into a seat, and stabilized.

Bly glanced around at the crowds coming in the rear doors. He looked over and saw Bill. "Bill, Bill," he called in delight, and raced up the aisle, working his way through a cluster of people to reach his old acquaintance. I saw him beaming with pleasure, leading Bill tenderly by the hand, back out of that row and down to a seat directly in front of the stage.

The reading began. It featured some talk on "Thirteen Ways of Looking at a Blackbird," the Wallace Stevens poem, some Kabir and Mirabai versions repeated to the dulcimer, a good deal of soapboxing. Bly was at the height of his popularity with the pagan counterculture and twenty or thirty minutes into the reading he got round to the topic of monotheism—in those days a subject he spent a great deal of time fulminating against. The audience was right with him, a crowd of brightly dressed longhair dopesmokers: surfers, organic farmers, college students, foresters, marine biologists, bakers. He snapped out a few jokes:

"I am an only God and a jealous God"

"Well if you're an only God what are you jealous of——?"

—and following the open vein, pilloried what he branded "monotheism." Jew, Christian, Muslim, didn't matter. They've had their day. Got to get past this thing with one god. Return to something colorful, pagan, friendly to women, full of mothers. He was enjoying himself, had his jokes at hand, and looked very pink up there under the lights in his flowered shirt, the dulcimer set on a little wood table. The freaks who'd come in from the mountains enjoyed him enormously, and there was something out of Tolkien about his appearance and his dulcimer poetry.

Suddenly Bly started, his eyes narrowing towards the rear of the hall. "Bill! Bill, where are you going?" Something broke. You could hear the seats creak as everyone strained to look back at the vanishing point towards which Bly stared in confoundment. And there went old Bill Everson, fleeing up the side aisle, cane clutched in one hand, arms swimming to keep him on his feet. It was almost slow motion, long hair and beard streaming back from under his broadbrimmed hat as he fled in a reflex of horror. "Bill…?" And Bill, muttering, muttering, eyes wild with terror, scarcely able to turn his old neck, managing to stammer out a few audible words, "Leaving, leaving, damn right, I'm leaving——"

Words drawn out with the keening I'd heard that day in the library. And the fury of a God he'd struggled thirty years with was surely flying alongside him. You don't need monotheism. Outside it was storming. In his buckskin jacket he looked feral and in the grip of some unknown panic. I thought I could see lightning dart from his beard. He crashed through the great double doors at the back of the church and was gone alone in the night.

Bly shuffled some papers, looking down hard. The hall was silent. Then in a considerably weakened voice read a brief poem with a surrealist bent. After which he sank straight back onto his chair, rubbed a hand over his face, and said in a quiet voice to no one in particular, "That was weird. Really, really weird."

Vidyā, the Sappho of India
(South India, ca. 8th century)

And what of those
arbors of vines
that grow where the river
drops away from Kalinda Mountain?
They conspired in the love
games of herding girls
and watched over the veiled
affairs of Rādhā.
Now that the days
are gone when I cut their
tendrils and laid them
down for couches of love,
I wonder if they've
grown brittle and if
their splendid blue flowers
have dried up.

No one really knows dates, or where exactly she lived. She belongs to a subterranean tradition, still only partly recovered, its documents scattered, most of its monuments looted by visiting armies over the centuries. She arose with the civilization of ancient India, and with its collapse virtually vanished. Yet Vidyā's poetry, its roots planted deep in the Paleolithic wildness of Asia, was nurtured in a culture of almost painful civility. There, among the courts of warlords with impeccable personal taste, far from the encampments of Europe, the most distinct woman of classical India wrote an unknown quantity of indelible verse. Fragments crop up now and then in anthologies, or old books of rhetoric quote with approval an elegant passage that no later poet's stylus has equaled. This has interested very few critics.

Beyond what little verse has been located, what do we know? One or two speculate she was a queen, but they've got nothing to go on. Some attribute to her and the renowned Kālīdāsa (who is survived by a number of plays and a great deal of poetry) a biting epigram, collaboratively written in old age, in which each finds pathetic a still-burning sexual hunger in the other's elderly body.

> *Distasteful*
> *a man with the stink of old age*
> *who can't get his*
> *thoughts off some girl—*
>
> *—or a withered woman*
> *tits sagging on an old paunch*
> *pulling a man*
> *towards her bed.*

There is no indication the two poets ever met. The same poem has been attributed to the poet Lady Shīlābhaṭṭarikā and a King Bhoja with no greater likelihood of accuracy.

At some point a British classicist with a good ear for poetry coined the phrase "Sappho of India." It's not a bad match. Vidyā is the earliest woman poet of Sanskrit, the clearest, the bravest. More poems attributed to her survive than of any other woman writing in Sanskrit and later critics, even the stiffest Brahmins, spoke of her with unrepentant admiration. Her sharply etched verse rings with passionate simplicity, the sort of poetry Sappho would have approved.

> *What wealth,*
> *that you can chatter*
> *about a night spent*

with your lover—
the teasings,
smiles, whispered words,
even his special fragrance.
Because O my friends I swear—
from the moment
my lover's hand touched my
skirt, I remember
nothing at all.

The poems that remain are all of the short *subhāṣita* type—individual lyrics. None of the recast epics, dramatic love cycles, or interlinked verse-forms other Indian poets went in for. Crisp image, Pound called it "the primary pigment of poetry," gives her verse classical strength. Each verse conjures something, some situation or emotion, that to go through means to be human. As though only a very short poem could contain so much living.

A highly educated woman of her day, Vidyā must have frequented some of the urbane courts and palaces where artists collected. Exquisitely cultured chieftains, often busy with warfare or civic duties, took time from their own art to establish such courts, and to host philosophers, musicians and literati. A few of these chieftains even wrote poetry of no little accomplishment. There was one ruler, no one knows his name or even the region he held, to whom Vidyā wrote a few tributes in verse. The cleverest of these—he must have been enormously charmed by it—parallels in playful, effortless images his military expertise to a lover's adroitness in bed. Written Sanskrit can be fashioned in a way that allows the eye to pick out two or more distinct sets of words from the same text, a bit like an optical illusion where by shifting focus two different images are seen. I'm not terribly fond of most of these—unless done well (and Vidyā's is) they seem more an exercise in gymnastics than in poetry.

Vidyā's best poems though, and we don't have many, look directly with a level eye on love. That eye, as quick to rural or even to wild landscapes as to sexual intricacies, took her to riverbanks, their thorns, wildlife, tangled

rushes. Flat stretches of sand, willow groves, catkins, whistling water
birds. Or into the mountains. Places lovers slip off to.

> On makeshift
> bedding in the cucumber
> garden, the hilltribe
> girl clings to
> her exhausted lover.
> Limbs still chafing
> with pleasure, dissolving
> against him she
> now and again with
> one bare foot
> jostles a cowry shell necklace
> that hangs from a
> vine on the fence—
> rattling it
> through the night,
> scaring the jackals off.

In the famous Sanskrit anthologies, put together between five and
eight centuries after her death, scholar-poets placed her poems of heart-
break in chapters called Separation of Lovers. Curiously, the poems of
"love tasted"—poems of bold, ardent women, who tasted their love one
suspects outside the arranged marriages that prevailed at the time—one
wonders what prompted the compilers to insert those under the heading
Faithless Women. To her poetic craft Vidyā was exactingly true.

> Dense downhanging branches,
> shade on the riverbank,
> dew on the wind—
> O Murala River—
> clear sand,
> whistling waterbirds,

who made your
willows such refuge,
a married woman
could come here for love,
undetected . . .

Though Vidyā walks with the planet's great women poets, one could spend a life reading and not come on her poems. A two volume anthology entitled *Women Writing in India: 600 B.C. to the Present,* edited by reputable feminist scholars and published by City University of New York in 1991 bypasses the Sanskrit poets entirely. In India, which has turned hopelessly puritanical since Vidyā's day, very few know her. She has all but vanished along with what must have been a terribly fine output of poems.

I got lucky once. A Muslim taxi driver in Calcutta, a mere scrap of paper with some quickly jotted directions to go on (which I could not read as they were in Bengali), helped me locate off the Bidhan Sarani a hole in the wall. A literal hole in the wall. From behind a few street vendor stalls I crouched through the gap where some very old masonry had been punched away, bent into an adjoining dark passage, cut several flights up an airless stone stairwell, and opened into an antiquarian book dealer's quarters. Old volumes, thousands of them under smoky light, stacked to the ceiling. The floors treacherous with books and old papers. No ascertainable order, just perilous column on column of books—Bengali, Oriyan, Hindi, Sanskrit, English. A white-haired man who seemed amused at being found out in his quarters flashed teeth reddened with betel and gave me to understand he could speak no English.

I pushed cautiously among his stacks while he rummaged for manuals on Tantra. It must have been instinct, but my hand pulled a tiny volume out from one heap: *Sanskrit Poetesses.* It had been published in Calcutta fifty years earlier and was threaded by wormholes. "Edited with critical notes, etc." The pages were foxed and tawny but the print glittered with sharp elegance, evidently the labor of someone who took pride in his job. I noticed a number of notes, pertaining to specific poems by the early women poets, made prim observations: "metre defective." The book contained this—I'd not seen it before—of the twenty-nine Vidyā poems which somehow get through the years to us:

To Her Daughter

As children we crave little boys,
pubescent we hunger
for youths,
old we take elderly men.
It is a family custom.
But like a penitent
you pursue
a whole life with one husband.
Never, my daughter,
has chastity
so stained our clan.

She must have lived to the south. In the north, a rigid system dominated by priests kept Sanskrit, that god-infested language of endlessly muttered ritual, from the ears and mouths of women. What frightened the Brahmins? Some god's displeasure, ink mixing poorly with motherhood? Unclean woman might spoil the buttermilk? Around Delhi, or north in the scholarly outpost of Kashmir, Vidyā would have been forbidden even to touch parchment or stylus. In the south things were easier. Women knew freedom and respect possibly left over from an earlier era.

Vidyā would have gone barefoot, barebreasted if you take the Gupta Dynasty's peerless sculpture as reflecting the way people clothed themselves; she would have had love affairs, worn jewels at her waistband, danced in silver anklets, carried children, swapped poems with her comrades. She loved men and had intimate girlfriends as well. This is all in the poems. When a lover deserted, she knew desolation, could cleanly give voice to her anguish—but not a life-threatening anguish. In the following poem she'd slip off to a riverside, and return excusing the little love-wounds alongside her nipples.

> *Neighbor, please*
> *keep an eye on my house*
> *for a moment.*
> *The baby's father*
> *finds our well water*
> *tasteless, and refuses*
> *to drink it. I'd better*
> *go, though alone,*
> *down to the river,*
> *though the thick*
> tamāla *trees and stands*
> *of broken cane*
> *are likely to*
> *scratch my breasts.*

A native of the south, her skin was certainly dark.

There's a verse of remarkable boldness, not like the love poems, one that fixes its gaze somewhere else. I don't think there's another like it in all of India. It shows she knew how remarkably good she'd become.

> *Not knowing me,*
> *Vidyā,*
> *dark as a blue lotus petal,*
> *the critic Daṇḍin*
> *declared Sarasvatī,*
> *goddess of verse-craft and learning,*
> *entirely white.*

Isha Upanishad

A Note on the Translation

Isha Upanishad IS A POEM, FIRSTLY A POEM.

Once when I wanted to read it with a group of students I found the existing translations unsatisfactory. Each had tried to reproduce its eighteen stanzas in the cautious, technical prose suited for philosophy. Not one had approached it as poetry—an insistent rhythmic poetry, mysterious as some pilgrim's stave, founded on tricky metrical changes, a fresh and savage grammar, fragments of old song, and the utterances of a lost dark prayer.

What had hampered the translations, I decided, was an inability to dwell in the uncertain. "An irritable reaching after fact or reason," as John Keats would put it, had distorted the various efforts in English. Even the formidable Indian commentators, ancient and modern, when they read *Isha* had done so with sectarian minds, unable to withstand the powerful and deliberate contrariness of the thing. As language raised into song, *Isha Upanishad* comes closer to music than to catechism.

For my translation I want to acknowledge the guidance of Professor Bhuwan Lal Joshi, friend, teacher, and a poet of the classroom at the University of California's Santa Cruz campus until his death in 1979. Himalayan by birth and upbringing, Tantric by temperament, he led me step by step through these stanzas. His own insights had been fed by the sādhus (wandering hermits), anti-monarchists, tribal priests, and Buddhist scholars who continue to animate his native Kathmandu Valley. He took to *Isha* as primal song—as though the contours of its stanzas were in no way separate from the mountains he'd grown up among. Yet he taught me to read it as territory native to myself. At the base of the coastal California mountains where we studied the stanzas in their tightly packed Sanskrit, they seemed brightly at home.

India's one hundred and eight *Upanishads* are a huge compendium of folklore, mystical insight, homespun humor, oblique anti-clerical dialogue, and wide open spaces for the mind. The verses of *Isha* ("The Great One") lie among their oldest strata. Scholars now place it in about the eighth century BCE. A few verses are surely rooted deeper than that, snatches of song from some very distant yogin, passed on as part of a large oral tradition and eventually (like the circulating lyrics of a blues song) brought to rest where they seemed to fit. Where the astute rhymes and troubling phrases all come from is anybody's guess. The carefully torqued dialectic, the cryptic accounts of work and learning, and their limits, all seem to echo from another life. The cry for a vision that nearly chokes on its own grammar in verse 16. Then the sober cremation verses that close it.

Who or what mind drew a thread, and strung the lyrics together? It arrives on the page still up-to-date after nearly three thousand years. Very scary, very nourishing stuff.

Isha Upanishad

1.

The Great One dwells
in all this, and in all
that moves in this mobile universe.
Enjoy things by
giving them up, not by craving
some other man's
substance.

2.

Engaged in works
hope to live
here for a hundred years—
it's what you receive,
nothing else.
There is no one for karma
to cling to.

3.

There are worlds
they call sunless,
turbulent,
covered with gloom—
those who
violate spirit
depart after death
into them.

4.

The Immobile One's
swifter than thought,
not even a god
can approach it.
Stands, yet outflanks what runs;
holds the waters
the Hidden Female let forth.

5.

Moves,
and does not move.
Is distant,
is near.
Inhabits all this,
stays outside of it all.

6.

Who sees
all breathing creatures
as self, self
in everything breathing,
no longer shrinks
from encounter.

7.

When the spectator
of this unity
regards all creatures as Self,
who can suffer,
who be misled?

8.

It is out traveling—
bright, bodiless, pure,
unflawed,
unbound by sinew,
unpierced by evil.
    All objects
have in their self-nature
been arranged precisely about us
by that presence—
poet, and thinker.

9.

They enter a turbulent
darkness, who
cultivate ignorance—
a yet thicker darkness
who are addicted to
knowledge.

10.

It is different
from knowledge—different also
from what you do not know—
this we heard
from the steadfast ones
who opened our eyes.

11.

Who is cunning
towards knowledge and ignorance,
with ignorance
moves across death,
with knowledge reaches
the deathless.

12.

They enter a turbulent
darkness, who
cultivate unmanifest ·worlds—
a yet thicker darkness
who are addicted
to empirical worlds.

13.

Different
from what you can see—
different also
from what goes unseen—
this we heard
from the steadfast ones
who opened our eyes.

14.

Who is cunning
towards loss and creation,
with loss
crosses death,
with creation reaches
the deathless.

15.

A golden solar disc
hides the gateway
into the Real—
remove it O Nourisher,
so I can see
the Unwavering.

16.

O Nourisher, sole Seer,
judge of the dead,
O sun, offspring of the Father of Creatures,
fan out your rays,
draw up lustre.
    That most
splendrous form, yours—
I would see—that is—
the *I am*

17.

Animate breath
   is undying
but the body ends in ashes.
Om!
   Oh volition, remember,
remember that which was done.
Remember
that which was
done.

18.

O Fire,
knower of every
   creature's breath,
take us along the good road,
far from deviant evil.
We offer you
   precious verse.

Lords & Ladies of Fructile Chaos
A Look at the Small Press

This essay began as a talk prepared for a panel entitled "The Small Press: Edit-ing, Publishing, Distributing," at The Jack Kerouac School of Disembodied Poetics, 22 July, 1991. Part of it was published in Talisman and reprinted in one of Small Press Distribution's yearly catalogues. Small Press Distribution, located in Berkeley, is the single most important distributor of contemporary poetry, fiction, and literary translation in the country. They handle more than 7000 titles—four hundred inde-pendent presses—from the United States, Mexico, Great Britain, and Canada. I found the happy phrase "Lords and ladies of Fructile Chaos" in an old notebook, cop-ied I think out of Milton. The entire range of publishing and bookselling is in rapid transition at the moment. The settlement in April, 2001, in which independent book-sellers were forced to drop their suit against the corporate chain booksellers bodes poorly for the free exchange of ideas in this country. Lawrence Ferlinghetti in the San Francisco Chronicle: *"The fat cats have won again." André Schiffrin's* The Business of Books, *published in 2000, provides a savvy insider's view of damage done to the book trade by the new corporate mentality. Though I think my own essay somewhat dated at this point, I reprint it as an artifact from an important moment in the ongoing struggle over information.*

WHAT COULD BE LESS compelling for an ordinary human than a discus-sion of the small press? By definition such talk would be concerned with the nuts and bolts of publishing: the blue and red pencils of editing, the transformation of raw manuscript into a marketable product, the diffi-cult stratagems of distributing and selling books. Wouldn't it largely be talk about creating needs where no need has existed, one basic premise of market capitalism? Isn't the Small Press after all a side show for people who have on their hands extra time (and not much of it), extra money (and very little of that); in other words isn't it a world of little shopkeepers? Populated by people who entertain odd, harmless and marginal hobbies?

Even sadder, might not the small press be a catch-all for pretenders to literature, a consolation for fledgling writers with not enough luck or talent to storm the gates of the Big Press? If you read what Kenneth Rexroth used to call "the liberal weeklies" this is the impression you're likely to get.

Let's start instead by saying that the so-called small press should be one of our most urgent concerns, not for writers and publishers only but for any intelligent person. What the small press is really about is information. There is no one living under our contemporary tyranny of knowledge—the control and misuse of information—who can discuss what it means to live freely, in the absence of what's termed the small press. Here are the relevant questions: What is information? How do we apply it in our lives? Who controls it, who fears its dissemination? How does it affect those with or without access to it? Only with access to a happily unrestrained flurry of intelligent publications can anyone hazard a reply.

So: what exactly is the small press? Let's go a step further and deny it's existence. *There is no such thing as the small press.* Not if you think of it as some established organization with card carrying members, or as an identifiable device made of iron, electricity, and ink; or as a licensed business operation with marketing and distribution departments. Small press is a catch-all term that points towards an unruly, confounding range of enterprises that produce and distribute printed information. These enterprises are decentralized, culturally alternative, minimally commercial, and often financially untenable. There is nothing unified about them, nothing particularly organized. Publishing operations can resemble guerrilla bands, formed for expediency around an intriguing artistic idea, a compelling social agenda, or a political issue, likely to disband when some other expediency calls. *Nor is there anything small about it.* Only from the viewpoint of Corporate Capital is the small press small. Only from the vantage of five or six enormous information conglomerates that control television networks, magazines, film studios, and publishing houses, does the small press seem diminutive. From any sane, decentralized vantage, the small press is the only show in town. Better, it is all the shows in town. It—they—these curious anti-centers of information which only by terrible accident produce a bestseller—are exactly what stand between the reading public and a considerable loss of free speech. What keeps the small press alive is its improbable, its *impossible* fecundity: diversity, enthusiasm, and financial recklessness.

With the appearance of corporate publishing—which came into its own immediately after World War II, and since the catastrophic economic shifts of the nineteen-eighties and nineties has been one limb of the information conglomerates—came the recognition that an entire populace could be stoned with disinformation, *and pay cash for it.* This had to give rise to some alternative, to an anarcho-bohemian underside, which continues to claw its way into existence, buying, borrowing, stealing, reclaiming or renovating the literal means of printed word production.

Remember, much as the dominant publishing houses would like you to believe it, the so-called small press is not a hobby for marginal or eccentric literary folk. Sadly, many respectable small houses have actually come to view themselves this way. On the contrary, it is the opposition to the dominant houses. *The small press is where you have to go if you want* information *that corporate publishing ignores or deliberately withholds.*

Information is of two very distinct and identifiable sorts. These might loosely correspond to Claude Lévi-Strauss's distinction between the raw and the cooked. They are: Direct Experience and Hearsay.

No hierarchy sets one above the other. Direct Experience is the foundation of individual consciousness. Hearsay comprises that lovely tangled complex, the cultural imagination. Maybe culture is the sum total at a given moment, among any unified social group, of Hearsay—all the collectively owned information which gets transmitted from person to person without having to be subjected to direct experience for verification. Hearsay information is carefully packaged, and transmitted with efficiency. It conserves time and effort since through it one learns much about one's world without having to directly visit the source.

However, with widespread literacy comes the fact that most hearsay is now distributed through print media. (I'll cautiously include the electronic media here, since it too is largely based on print and literacy.) For citizens, this implies a terrible vulnerability to either state or corporate interests now that the major print media have fallen into the hands of the few people wealthy enough to run the show. Fortunately there is hearsay important to each of us that comes through the independent small publishers. Here's a partial list of topics from books I've used over the past few decades. Some may look dated but in their own day seemed very revolutionary indeed. This list should demonstrate that hearsay does not mean "of secondary importance."

> How to fix an old VW or Honda at home.
> What the perils of infant vaccines are, and what alternatives
> your family has.
> How to grow dope in your closet.
> How to treat specific diseases without recourse to surgery
> or costly drugs.
> Why law enforcement agencies have killed members of AIM and
> the Black Panthers.
> What military hardware the U.S. sells and to whom.
> How to protect yourself against AIDS.
> How to defend yourself in court; or from car salesmen; or against
> a rapist.
> How to monkeywrench and otherwise protect public land from
> corporate harvesting.
> The way international money operates.
> How to train groups in non-violent civil disobedience.
> How to form a watch-dog committee on a local police force.
> And so forth . . . including . . . how to start a small press.

The advent of the Internet probably doesn't change the need for books. Printer and poet William Everson used to say the book is an *archetype*, meaning it is deeply established in the human psyche. Humans have lived with it in one form or another for several thousand years. It fits the hand; some of the best fit the hip pocket; it does not require electricity and makes no noise; it provides a quiet refuge; it is not going to go away soon. Book publishing will continue, augmented in numerous ways by computers. In fact the rise of the home computer and widespread use of the internet has been accompanied by a quiet resurgence of fine letterpress printing. Since the nineteen sixties, pioneer printers like Adrian Wilson, Clifford Burke, Kathy Kuehn, and Wesley Tanner have led a noiseless but effective book renaissance, demonstrating how often one looks to the past to design the future.

Why might a resurgence of handcrafted books, meant among other motives to slow down the speed of production and reading, have occurred? Any musings will take me to the conviction that there exists, beyond hearsay, direct experience available through books. Here is where "literature" comes into the picture. Reactionary forces seem more incensed by these books, which if I'm right transmit experience directly, than they are by books of hearsay. Or why has it been largely works of poetry and fiction that come under the assault of state-sponsored censorship? From *Ulysses* and *The Tropic of Cancer* to *Howl* and Lenore Kandel's *The Love Book,* fiction and poetry seem to provide something direct. Maybe they transmit key information about values, about how you live a life of commitment, love, humor, brilliance. To use a term of Gregory Bateson's, they provoke metalearning. When what you read does not simply tell about something but shifts how you conduct your life, isn't that direct experience?

The anarchic arena called the small press is in fact the dancing ground for much *transcribed* hearsay and most *inscribed* direct experience, all of it the sort corporate houses have not found it in their interests to publish. Definitions are slippery here, and boundaries indistinct. In poetry and fiction, what was once brought public by the small press, through changes of social or historical consciousness sometimes gets popular and a corporate publishing house sees an opportunity for profit or prestige by picking up the title. There also exist in-between presses. It is a good thing no hard and fast boundaries exist. It means information lives like a nomad, it's on the hoof, it *moves.* And it changes consciousness.

Without defining it precisely, without defining it at all, everyone involved in the small press knows what it is, how it operates, what value it holds, and what threatens it. Want a definition? Then let's define Big Press.

Let's call *that* the voice of Capital. Let's say one of the things it does is establish *fraudulent & marketable substitutes for hearsay & direct experience.*

There are a number of serious dangers facing the small press. The much celebrated cutback in NEA funds, the fulminations of Jesse Helms and his ilk, as well as the overall streamlining of grants and awards toward mainstream projects, do not pose the grave or immediate danger. The greatest peril is loss around the country of independent bookstores to corporate chains. Knowledgeable independent booksellers are pivotal culture workers. They continue a long line of brave scholars, willing to stock shelves, to hustle good books, sometimes even to publish them; without their efforts we will all die with no readers and no worthwhile books to read. This is what is very likely to occur in not too many years. What will be lost? I wrote the following for the *St. Marks Poetry Project Newsletter* (1999) when I heard City Lights Books in San Francisco had swung a surprise deal to purchase their old wooden historical building and save the choice real estate turf from becoming a bank or a fancy restaurant:

Certainly the most storied bookshop in the country. Still as good, and as radically diversified as any. Literature, classics, politics, poetry, ecology. Volume after volume. Not a crummy bestseller among 'em. Loans will help buy the building, as well as perform an earthquake retrofit—iron girders so the old wood-and-plaster building won't collapse while you're digging through anarchist tracts in the basement or for some comrade's recent poetry title upstairs.

Nothing beats their creaky dim-lit upstairs triangular poetry room. Funny angled walls stuffed with the century's best. They hold book-party readings there too. About eight chairs fit onto the old wood floor, but somehow a few dozen people squeeze in to hear poetry. Surely the place is one holy pilgrimage site.

Across the street bronze plaque on a brick wall commemorates The Condor, world's first topless bottomless dancer club. What about a plaque for City Lights, first paperback store in the country? Publisher of *Howl*, of Kerouac, di Prima, Snyder, of contemporary Mexican, Cuban and Bosnian writers, of too many historic titles to list? I couldn't see one.

Remember a day when giants walked the earth, and a few booksellers cared so much for literature that they published the books? Only a dishonorable person would buy from Barnes & Noble or Borders when real places—City Lights, Shambhala, The Grolier Bookshop, still exist. Tell your children!

Chain bookstores swing sweetheart deals with corporate publishers, hence purchase flashy merchandise at great discount, hence sell at artificially low prices. They would have readers believe that if you paid fair market value for a book you'd been ripped off. Unable to compete on mainstream books and bestsellers (on which every bookstore even the most idealist must make enough dough to pay the rent) independents fold. This has particularly occurred in newly fashionable urban neighborhoods. Chain stores regularly move with predatory intent into neighborhoods that already support a bookstore.

All this is very simple, very obvious, and requires no analysis. The chain stores are not hiding it. Of threats to the small press this is the most serious: it is justified and legalized by free market capitalism. One can only laud the booksellers who are fighting back, in court and elsewhere, to preserve the energetic clash and flow of information. Mimeo machines of the sixties in basements, photocopy machines of the seventies, restored hand presses and garage-sale type cabinets of the eighties, Aldus Pagemaker of the nineties with its joyous access to type fonts, unnamed desktop innovations of the future; these have stood in the ranks as our guardians of Wild Form and Savage Grammar. With them stand the independent booksellers, our dear Lords and Ladies of Fructile Chaos.

Notes On Form & Savage Mind

---

for Robin Blaser and Joanne Kyger

Proem

EVERY AGE BURNS INCENSE TO ITS GODS.

In our own day, about eleven millennia since the worldwide retreat of the glaciers and the end of the Pleistocene, the human realm is alight with prophecies. Priests of the Age of Information—from new age Third Wave Speakers of the House to electronic energy-web anarchist computer hackers—are declaring that the human species stands at some threshold of social and possibly genetic evolution. Certainly the multinational corporations of resurgent late twentieth century Capitalism adhere to this very particular mythology.

The new mythos, breaking with the stories of Christianity, Buddhism, and Islam, as well as regional and tribal faiths, holds forth the freshly minted figure of corporate warrior as American archetype. It promises breathtaking electronic and biotechnology capabilities for the immediate future. A few of its more far out visionaries even suggest an eventual liberation from old age, sickness and death. Current vocabulary has taken a new, deliberate inflection, applying information science terminology to nearly every aspect of life, including personal relationships.

But has civilization entered a major historic phase, the age of Information? Will disembodied mind free itself of biological limits? Will genetic engineering make up for the depletion of earth's forests and fossil fuels or the final harvesting of the seas?

Look around you. I'm going to start by making the assertion that as a species living in history, we have never left the Bronze Age. It is possible, following the classic categories of archaeology, that we've progressed into an Iron Age, but that would be only a slightly more efficient extension of the age of bronze weapons and burnished religious icons. Age of steam, age of discovery, age of industry, the same basic principals hold. For all the clever innovative technologies and methods of thought, the species continues to live in a period dominated by hard metals, dogmatic political or military leaders, and rigid hierarchies. A brief visit to the planet's so-called developing countries, or a survey of Eastern Europe after the collapse of their communist governments, ought to show the extent to which most human lives still revolve around several basic truths: the economics of food scarcity, the degradation of the natural world, and the hazards of metal weaponry.

Let me give a quick structural identity to what we call Civilization. It covers a time span of approximately eight or ten thousand years. During this period, which seems to arise with agriculture and animal husbandry and the novel ability to stockpile wealth, our planet has seen a progressive development of the war-economy State, the establishment of social and military hierarchies, the rise of organized churches, and the creation of internal police forces by which the State controls its own people. There has also been the progressive separation of an educated urban elite, which tends to concentrate wealth, from the local populaces and bioregions which provide the material source of that wealth.

Within this context, the interests of a few of us return again and again to the hold-outs, the renegades or misfits, the folk who cast up some concerted resistance to these mainstays of Bronze Age mental habits. Such people manage to retain, alongside the recent or *metallic* casts of mind, a mode of thinking anthropologist Claude Lévi-Strauss designated "savage mind." Lévi-Strauss predicated *la pensée sauvage*, this older way of thinking, on close observation of the natural world and a swift metaphorical imagination grounded in what could loosely be called natural history. In our contemporary historical period he located hold-outs for savage thinking among the company of artists. "Art," said Lévi-Strauss—by now it has been quoted many times—"is a National Park for the mind."

I.

Some serviceable tools were handed us during the nineteenth century, primarily by naturalists, ethnologists, and other hip non-dogmatic observers of our biotic planet, which helped crack apart several key assumptions of Bronze and Iron Age thinking. While these scientists and explorers (most of them amateurs) rode a modern secularist crest of thought, much that they brought to view hearkened back to pre-Bronze Age underpinnings. An older, perhaps saner, human view of the world and one's place in it—never entirely absent but for millennia driven underground—began to assert itself. Bronze Age cultures had known these ways of employing the mind, but generally found them scary, weird, a bit too fast, loose, and sexy. Too unpredictable, and therefore resistant to state or religious control.

What sort of tools or methods of thought? Probably not too distant from what characterized Paleolithic world-views, and which provided the Neolithic its energetic "arts of civilization" (Lévi-Strauss's term again). These arts included the domestication of plants and animals, brewing, agriculture, pottery, weaving—and their origins are not well understood. During the nineteenth century perceptual tools appear in the writings of Darwin, Thoreau, and several dozen other writers who in heroic ways begin to reintroduce a bit of savage mind to Western civilization. Gradually separating themselves from anthropocentric habits of belief, they reverted to careful observation of the natural world as human habitat and began to record their observations in unusual modes of writing. Noting how Nature's keen, shape-shifting laws govern the human animal as well as its fellow biological creatures, they prepared the path for what's sometimes called eco-centric or bio-centric thought.

Part of this return to old-time habits emerged from a reconfigured art of ethnography. Anthropology in its formative period was an applied colonialist science, its mandate simply to provide Europeans with some pragmatic guidelines for ruling peoples who exhibited widely divergent cultural traits. As it struggled to become a more disinterested mode of study it turned into something radically, even ruthlessly different—a sharp reflexive look at the particular culture that spawned it. "Anthropology is the critique of progress," wrote Octavio Paz, himself an inveterate traveler, ambassador to India for the Mexican government during the 1960s, and a keen observer of non-Western cultures.

Ethnographic reports have brought into consciousness the dizzying array of cultures and possible social forms distributed across our planet. Some of this report had been arriving for centuries, in the accounts of travelers who studied firsthand the confounding diversity of cultures beyond Europe's borders, and learnt something subtle about the "made up" qualities of each. Was it Robert Duncan who said man is not just the creature who makes things, but the one who makes things up?

In the wakening arts of ethnography, natural history, and biodiversity studies, Marco Polo stands out as a secret hero—the first steady-eyed and discriminating ethnographer to produce a widely read book in Europe since Herodotus. He brought back from Asia to thirteenth century Italy report of human possibilities way beyond what the "mind of Europe" was ready to take in. Outlandish peoples, wildly disparate language systems, local gods and spirits, colorful habits of dress, divergent definitions of marriage and kinship, a bright chaos of plant, bird, and animal life. Today anyone who's lived in a North American city has some firsthand exposure to this kind of complexity, but in Polo's day it took a remarkable leap to accept it. Emanuel Komroff's Introduction to his good edition of the *Travels* (a field guide that carefully distinguishes direct observation from hearsay, but known in Polo's own day as a Book of Marvels) recounts the story of Polo on his death bed. Marco's many friends had clustered around—all upstanding Christian businessmen who had grown prosperous on trade to the Levant. Concerned about their companion's soul after death, and never wavering for an instant from their certainty that his book was a hodge-podge of fanciful stories invented for reasons they did not understand, they urged Polo to retract the fabulous observations he had recounted. His answer—

I have not told half of what I've seen.

Allegiance to the seeing eye as against the dogmatic mind. It came forcefully forward with renegade naturalists and solitary geologists, reaching some flashpoint in the nineteenth century. Darwin and others—it seems to have dawned in a number of minds at about the same time—began to gaze deeply into the physical world of which they were part, freeing themselves from the reigning theologies—and saw what most aboriginal peoples had known. What a few Asiatic traditions like Taoism, or certain occult traditions in the West, had kept in sight: the swift mutability of the world, its species and creatures.

This was terribly exciting to observe! It suggested possibilities of kinship among creatures that must have been lost when hunting vanished as a regular practice and the secret of domestication disappeared (in historical times no significant new animal has been domesticated). Along with the staggering picture of evolutionary kinship, every species and every individual's identity altered. Species after Darwin, no longer regarded as eternal "forms" created by a rigid intelligence, became open, shapeshifting, creative events. Performances or epic journeys. Every species makes itself up. Not necessarily by deliberate choice, certainly not at the whims of distinct individuals, but in a manner of deep slow experimentation. For humans who make poetry the enterprise began to change too. Robin Blaser, master poet for many decades & now a kind of American poet laureate in exile to Canada, describes in his work, "a principle of *randonnée*—the random and the given of the hunt, the game, the tour."

Not a new way of thinking, but one inestimably old and regularly renewed: that the cosmos, or this Earth, does not hide some actual self behind appearances, but works out laws—you could say reveals itself, body, speech, and mind—through all that appears and changes. Weather patterns, geological transformations, flora and fauna, bird flight, the shifting of continents, the birth and death of mountains. These are the tracks of instinct, the windings of complicated thought, or a far-reaching grammar.

...the random and the given of the hunt, the game, the tour.

For a resident of the temperate North American continent, the writings of Henry David Thoreau might stand as an example in poetry that works out the implications of Darwin's insights. Thoreau only read Darwin's *The Descent of Species* at the end of his life, but his own observations made him fully prepared for the implications. The *Journals* he kept for over twenty years (fourteen volumes in their new Princeton University press incarnation) work out massively, confoundingly, the principles of *randonnée*. Thoreau permitted his own "hunts, games, and tours," daily walks of four or more hours, to determine the structure of his writing. His *Journals* meet the random and the given head on. Or, to make it a bit more ordinary, call it chance encounters, what-the-world-presents. Just as evolving species encounter what's out there, and genetically inscribe over time their most successful responses, Thoreau at the quicker pace of a human life built a set of writings determined by encounters with the native orders around Concord, Massachusetts.

Having no model for what he was writing, it must have come painfully upon Thoreau, over many years, that his *Journals* were gradually becoming something other than raw material from which to quarry passages for his books. Today many of us read them as the central project of his life:

> . . . *thoughts written down thus in a journal might be printed in the same form with greater advantage—than if the related ones were brought together in separate essays. They are now allied to life—& are seen by the reader not far fetched—It is more simple—less artful.*

A poem or a journal like a species: no longer immutable.

Thoreau's hard-won insights are now ground for a particularly North American creed. It would state that Cosmos reveals itself in the form and flux of tectonic upheavals, in the tender intricacies of ecology and the evolution of species, in meteorological patterns of occurrence and recurrence, and in the welter of events from the human sphere. Daily encounters with one's own patterns of thought, and attention to world events as they unfold, enter the field. Entering, they alter it. If the governing principle is mutability prompted by random encounters, then the characteristic of literature must also be emergent, open, shifty, organic, projective. Could this be what Thoreau meant by *wild*?

Not for strength, but for beauty, the poet must, from time to time travel the
logger's path and the Indian's trail, to drink at some new and more bracing
fountain of the muses, far in the recesses of the wilderness.

II.

To know the mind of a yogin or adept—say a Zen roshi or Vajrayāṇa
tulku—the student takes on the master's discipline. The malleable human
mind gathers its shape from the uses it's put to. One might accordingly—
to know the mind of Thoreau and how he cocked a sceptical humorous eye
at the world's pageant—practice his discipline—the walker's journal. An
eyeblink and it's Bashō. He listens to wind tear at the roof of his banana leaf
hut. A driving rain pours in runnels. Can you hear the ancestors in the
wind?

A practice of journal, or poem-as-journal. A way to track events of the
journey. A journey we now know from the insights of ecology to be larger
than the history of nations, larger than human philosophies, or industry, or
war. Larger than the journey of our own species. In the geological record
now being studied, *Homo sapiens sapiens* takes a late role. My naturalist
friend Peter Warshall has been at work for a decade on the "four billion
year history of aesthetics." He asks questions like why a stop sign is red, or
a valentine card. Curiously, the likeliest answer may be found in the structure of the seeing eye. The eye as it has developed through a succession of
species, for several hundred million years, on a green oxygen-rich planet.

A profusion of plant and animal observations wander into Thoreau's
Journal, particularly after 1851, and dominate his writings until the end of
his life. No less the taste of the scientific Latin terms Thoreau digs up for
each plant or animal he meets. Words as often as creatures he tracks into
far off lairs. He lifts an old Spanish term, *grammatica parda*—and lends it
New England life: tawny grammar. He's wrestling with Linnaeus and old
human traditions of language use, but he's also taken to words in order to
more actively meet events. *Journal* is the site of learning, the autodidact's

form of memory. A particularly literate extension of the old practice of naming, which our species uses to find its way in the world.

Gertrude Stein calls poetry "a vocabulary entirely based on the noun." "That is poetry really loving the name of anything."

And Ernest Fenollosa: "Poetry agrees with science and not with logic."

Kshemendra, a twelfth century poet, yogin, and raconteur from Kashmir, specifies the skills a poet should cultivate.

> With his own
> eyes a poet
> observes the shape of a leaf.
> He knows how to make
> people laugh
> and studies the nature of each living thing.
> The features of ocean and mountain,
> the motion of sun, moon, and stars.
> His thoughts turn with the seasons.
> He goes among
> different peoples
> learning their landscapes,
> learning their languages.

I'd salt this short list with a bit more environmental literacy:

> animals & seasons
> their habits & rutting behavior
>
> rules of the local authorities.

By local authorities I don't firstly mean elected officials or employees of government. These folk do their particular and necessary jobs; but past them, out in the brush, lie other folk who "make" laws too. I refer to what Sanskrit speakers called *lokapāla*, local protectors. We might say tutelary deities. These creatures, biologically real and deeply imaginary at the same time, hang on in the popular mind as mascots and emblems, even for people who've never met one. The best lokapālas are what conservation biologists call " indicator species" or "keystone species"—creatures so precisely and intricately woven into their local ecology that disruptions of order which haven't yet begun to appear widely can be registered in their shifting behavior or decline in health.

To cherish the *lokapālas*
      cougar & coyote
        mule deer
    black tail prairie dog & his predator red tail hawk
who dwell year round among us
      —or such who pull into high country when
          summer sun opens krumholz
           & tundra—
for winters might drop to the plains
      or go
      "underground"
      quiet the metabolism
          plug the digestive track
Others arrive seasonally
long range migratory folk—
these ones also precious in the post-DDT era
    birds who breed at high latitudes
        come as colorful singing guests to our brief but
    "insect rich arctic summer"

Might we consider them "ours"?
    More accurate to say

      "southern species"

on a brief foray north to get protein & breed.

Change, individuation, metamorphosis. Migration, shapeshifting, transmogrification. All point towards growth itself, not the grown thing, as the basis. Poet-scholars of the late twentieth century, schooled in biological studies and armed with sharp taxonomic skills, add to Kshemendra's list what can be learnt of *metabolism*—a flux of inward sugar production, complicated food chain relationships, and invisible energy webs. Despite their functional precision, any creature's metabolism operates so far outside human observation as to seem nearly indeterminate.

III.

In the dream I take pen to the journal. Noting down words as they arrive. "Nature is growth, change, metamorphosis." *Transmutation of form* appears on the page. A principle the Chinese call *ch'i*, the Hindus *prāna*. "Not measurable." Further words crawl forward. "Growth itself, not the thing grown." The surrounding landscape is dry desert, tawny and cracked, littered with black volcanic cones. Prevalent vegetation is sagebrush—*artemisia*—grey-blue leathery leaves replicating a grey cast of sky. A ramp of cobblestones with masonry railings "dilapidated"—meaning "stone by stone coming apart"—remnants of some former civilization. Down an adjoining staircase of precarious stonework, hence "picking" their way, come Anne & Ambrose. I look up from the page, the words then counsel: do not abandon *the human realm.*

What if the journal were to get written in dream? Writing inscribe what sleep guardedly shows? Sanskrit *svapna* means both sleep and dream, a single activity. What was archaic India's understanding of dream? For Presocratic Greece, Dodds quotes various sources—not as we would say, *I had a dream*

but *I saw a dream.*

Closer than most philosophies get. Dream like evolutionary theory predicates shapeshifts and transformations. It's just that the dream works quicker. Two Teton Sioux dream songs as recorded by Frances Densmore—

friend
my horse
flies like a bird
as it runs

        some one
        told me
        a Wolf nation
        called me "father"

Massachusetts, 1630, introduces the first animal bounty in the New World—a shilling for every wolf carcass. By 1837 wolves have vanished from Connecticut. From New Hampshire by 1895, the Adirondacks by 1899. By 1909 they are gone from the forests of Maine.

Wolf was once the most widely distributed land mammal on Earth.

Thoreau, 26 June 1851, after a visit to a traveling "menagerie"—

> *I was struck by the gem-like changeable greenish reflections from the eyes of the grizzly bear— So glassy that you never saw the surface of the eye— They quite demonic. Its claws though extremely large & long look weak & made for digging or pawing earth & leaves. It is unavoidable the idea of transmigration not merely a fancy of the poets— but an instinct of the race.*

Transmigration an instinct?

Unseen bird calls harshly a hundred yards off. In foothills below Arapahoe Pass "from about 9,500 feet down to the plains, is a rather extensive network of ancient trails, many of which follow the same routes as present day roads" (R.L. Ives, "Early human occupation of the Colorado headwaters region." Geographical Review, 1942).

I revisit a few pages of Thoreau's *Journal* and find entered "After January 10, 1851" an account of his going "down cellar just now to get an armful of wood," where he heard "methought a commonplace suggestion—but when as it were by accident—I reverently attended to the hint—I found that it was the voice of a God who had followed me down cellar to speak to me." The passage turns out to be not about a God but an act of attention—

How many communications may we not lose through inattention?

I would fain keep a journal which should contain those thoughts & impressions which I am liable to forget that I have had. Which would have, in one sense the greatest remoteness—in another the greatest nearness, to me.

A moment stolen by chance from inattention. On 19 August, 1851 he observes—

The poet must be continually watching the moods of his mind as the astronomer watches the aspects of the heavens. What might we not expect from a long life faithfully spent in this wise—the humblest observer would see some stars shoot.—A faithful description as by a disinterested person of the thoughts which visited a certain mind in 3 score years & 10 as when one reports the number & character of the vehicles which pass a particular point.

A meteorological journal of the mind—

13 MAY 1995

In the dream I have gathered up pages for a collection of early Buddhist poetry we are translating. The sheets are small strips of bark or leaf— "prepared palm leaves" ca. 80 BCE, Śri Lanka. They fit the hand awkwardly, a thick unmanageable bundle. Anne delivers to me her latest revisions on strips the belly color of a purple martin. "Leafing" through I see illustrations, not text—skeletal figures arranged in erotic postures, *Citāpati* graveyard figures of the Tibetan sort. Others emerge in delicate pastel washes—

flat landscapes, forlorn women, the colors and intricate draft-work recall miniature paintings of the Rajput hill schools. Some could be Attic Greek, ivory & cobalt blue, ladies with robes opening over adolescent breasts— want to know how they got on the palm leaf. Did someone use computer graphics to transfer them? The oldest technology, ochre & charcoal—& the most recent—merge in the writing—

The one dictum upon which Natural Selection insists: genetic muta- tion and evolutionary change proceed by what we call *chance operation*. The grand play of forms evolving through four billion years, transmigration of species from structure to structure, habit to habit, homeland to homeland. Form to form. No grand authority determines the shifts and feints, pat- terns of the farfalla's wing, stripes that lend a tiger's face distinction. Eye color, fin shape—we stand free of any terrible dominant intelligence. And are given over to the play of encounter, the aleatoric gesture, the curve of an eyebrow the poets of India likened to Kāma's bow.

From Joseph Needham's *Science and Civilization In China*, a chapter heading: "The Chinese Denial of a Celestial Lawgiver an Affirmation of Nature's Spontaneity & Freedom."

Heaven has no form and yet the myriad things are brought to perfection.

This may be called the untaught teaching,
            the wordless edict.

IV.

The early Buddhists prized a meditation on the body and its imperma- nence. The practice: to visualize one's own impending decay. The vaporous body, hissing from broken fissures, wet with lesions, ingested in mouthfuls by worm or jackal or feral dog. It is a grim vigilance, the recommended site of practice the burial ground. One studies a corpse breaking open from heat and bacterial moisture; holding up the mirror of Buddha's teach- ing one regards it as one's own, an eye-blink away in time.

There is another meditation though, vastly older and strikingly more up-to-date. I find it displayed in the work of the best minds of the past 150 years applying themselves to a no less rigorous, an equally non-sentimental observation. This is to stare past the revulsion of decay, the fear of body and its changing qualities. To observe one's own elements not "dead" but taken back to the play of life forms—by worm or ant, sifted down to compost or detritus. Not fear but eternal delight—buzzard or blue jay, blue gramma or Doug fir, microscopic organisms tracing the subsoil, flank of a deer off the highway.

In the intricate weave of protoplasm, the patterned weave of the biotic fabric, old myth sees a transmigration of souls. With hard cold looking one observes that it's not just the human realm, not just "us" on the journey. All is exchange, mutation, migration of cellular nutrients. No wonder generosity is highly prized in most cultures.

> *It is unavoidable the idea of transmigration not*
> *merely a fancy of the poets—but an instinct of the race.*

Can the dream with its litter of barkless twig and owl pellet show a way through? The Mahāyāna Buddhist believes we have all been fellow travelers on a beginningless journey through such intricacies of rebirth, and for so long, that each of us has taken or will take on every form, every shape, every species. Contemporary scientists can study the periodicity by which each cell of the body replaces itself, or each molecule of water passes through a given watershed. For this reason the Bodhisattva does not rest until every sentient creature has come to its own awakening, down to the smallest blade of grass. Old Buddha's documents mention the "deva eye" capable of seeing one's previous incarnations. To peer through that lens, I am certain, would illuminate a Burgess Shale of lifeforms.

Darwin, closing *The Origin of Species*—

There is grandeur in this view of life, with its several powers, having been originally breathed into a few forms or into one; and that, whilst this planet has gone cycling according to the fixed law of gravity, from so simple a beginning endless forms most beautiful and most wonderful have been, and are being, evolved.

And Herakleitos, old poet of savage mind—

> One must talk about everything according to its nature,
> how it comes to be and how it grows.

T'ao Ch'ien's Withered Wood Poetry

WHEREVER *vihāras* or Buddhist practice-centers develop, they seem to attract a loose-knit collection of poets who come and go through their hallways. What some of these poets write is distinctly flavored by Buddhist ideas. Wit, subtle metaphysical insight, and iconic imagery they've picked up in their wanderings flashes throughout. With others the influence stays hidden. You need to read closely, so ordinary and spontaneous seem their depictions of tenderness, impermanence, or solitude. This tacit Buddhist influence appears with a distinct flavor in a few of the poets of old India, but too little is known of those ancients to say much about their lives and their poetry. It is the Chinese poet T'ao Ch'ien (365-427) who appears as the first formidable personality to demonstrate this loose and affectionate connection to Buddhism.

Not coincidentally, T'ao is also the poet who first used that "bland and withered" voice which gives the best-known Chinese poetry a candor and simplicity unmatched until certain twentieth century poets hit on something similar. T'ao lived through a turbulent and politically insecure period in Chinese history. Military power in his day swung back and forth between a succession of warriors and regents, their tactics as ruthless as they were opportunistic. The only vocation available to a man of letters, that of official bureaucrat, struck T'ao early on as morally compromised given the period's politics, as well as impossibly dangerous. Looking back from a later vantage he mused,

> Why live like all those fine men, hearts
> stuffed with fire and ice to the end,
>
> their hundred-year return to the grave
> nothing but an empty path of ambition?

The records are too scant to get a sense of what his work was while in office. Given the dangerously shifting political ground, any too evident ambition or the assumption of even a modest role in actual government would have been markedly unsafe. So after trying to keep his head above water in various minor positions for a bit more than a decade, he retired to his family village in South China, six miles from the provincial capital of Hsun-yang, and close by the Yangtze River. He adjusted to a life of hard outdoor work. Subsistence farming presented him a different set of worries, but let him cultivate a few friends in obscurity, raise a family to which he was devoted, and to take close note with an artist's eye as the seasons passed. At this time he stopped using his given name, T'ao Yuan-ming, and assumed the name Ch'ien which means "the retiring." Ch'ien the recluse was how he wished to be known: Ch'ien who isn't available. Ch'ien who drinks wine and pursues what he calls idleness (hsien). Who drinks wine when it's available, to sharpen his perceptions and write poetry for his own amusement.

> I live in town without all that racket
> horses and carts stir up, and you wonder
>
> how that could be. Wherever the mind
> dwells apart is itself a distant place.

It was of this poetry—about 125 poems have come through the centuries to us—that a later poet, Huang T'ing-chien, declared, "When you've just come of age, reading these poems is like gnawing on withered wood. But reading them after long experience in the world, it seems the decisions of your life were all made in ignorance." It's a particular tone that many subsequent poets adopted: secular, circumspect, modest, and full of historical detail:

> Life soon returns to nothing. The ancients
> all said it circles away like this. And if
>
> Sung and Ch'iao ever lived in this world
> without dying, where are they now?

"Still," T'ao continues in the same poem—a touch of mischief and wit preventing his deeply sober thought from getting maudlin—"my old neighbor swears his wine makes you immortal, so I try a little…."

T'ao's farm lay slightly north of Lu Mountain, a storied landmark which dominates the region. Nearby his farm and associated with the mountain stood a Buddhist monastery, quite celebrated in the early years of Chinese Buddhism due to its singularly energetic abbot, Hui-yuan. T'ao struck up a friendship with Hui-yuan—a sort of proto-Zen teacher who dispensed various Pure Land visualization and chanting techniques while basing his principal practice at Lu Mountain on *dhyāna*, meditation. What later evolved into Ch'an (Zen) Buddhism had early roots here. Hui-yuan, the records also tell us, used Taoist terminology to clarify Buddhist concepts for his students—one of the consequential steps on the way to a Buddhism distinctly Chinese in approach.

Evidently sharpened by certain yogic practices, T'ao occasionally takes himself off in his poems to some quiet spot, "settling into my breath." But his poems remain rooted in a pragmatic and no-nonsense Taoism—the Taoism of Lao Tzu or Chuang Tzu. He delights in the term *tzu-jen*, which means something like "after one's own nature," or "spontaneous," giving it a central role in his thought, and making him seem astonishingly contemporary with writers and painters of New York in the 1950s, or San Francisco in the sixties. One can't help wishing some record remained of the conversations he had with his Buddhist friend—the vigorous abbot hammering out an approach to Buddhism distinctly Chinese, the reclusive poet shrewd enough to shake off the life of a government bureaucrat and pursue a Way founded on the natural orders.

They say

a single generation and, court or market,
every face is new. It's true, of course.

Life is its own mirage of change.

How much does the "withered wood" flavor of T'ao Ch'ien's poetry owe to his friend's Buddhist instructions? Probably not much. The chanting he speaks of as a singular delight in some poems is probably on most occasions no more than the traditional method of reciting scholarly verse to the lute-like *ch'in*. There are reports that Hui-yuan introduced wine-drinking at his monastery in order to tempt T'ao Ch'ien into joining the order, but monastic life after all is quite alien to *tzu-jen*, full of terribly arduous work and the tough job of harmonizing a variety of distinct personalities. Observing the willows that grew near his house, and which figure enormously in later stories of his life, T'ao declared one should not emulate them, bowing all the time: the wind gusts and they bow this way, the wind gusts again and they bow that way. That's fine for willows but for people, "One bow for five sacks of rice," a more reasonably proportioned behavior. So T'ao the retiring followed his path of hard outdoor work, worrisome children, wine when he could afford it, leisure when he could get it, and poetry.

> Has anyone come into this world without
> leaving it? Life will always end. At home
>
> in what lasts, I wait it out. A bent arm
> my only pillow, I keep emptiness whole.

Much as he appreciated the monastery near his farm and the companionship of its innovative and lettered abbot, T'ao did not need or hanker after its discipline. He followed an older stricter Way, and did not much complain about putting it to practice. *Tzu-jen*—the same religion the geese and cicadas of his poetry follow—or the trees and clouds. "One's own nature." All the books speak of how close it is to a person, but how difficult to put into practice. Is this true? For a human—once you've stripped away cumbersome theologies, ranks of divinities, layers of ritual, and all the other trappings of organized religion—it simply means cultivating the vigilance and tenderness which arise with an awareness of death. Watching your own mind, acting in accord with your neighbors, staying on friendly terms with local plants and animals, enjoying one's family. This is the practice. It must be the oldest religion, and the simplest. Add the occasional evening with a dear friend, a few cups of wine, some seasoned poetry—and you've got a very civilized life indeed.

> At sunset, light fading slowly away, I linger
> fondly over a lone pine, nowhere I'd rather be.

The best current translations are those by David Hinton. His book of T'ao Ch'ien's poetry includes the terse, ironic note T'ao Ch'ien wrote on himself. Tao had modeled it on early biographic sketches by the Chinese historians, giving it a flavor at once archaic and richly ironic. "He was a wine-lover by nature, but couldn't afford it very often... He must have lived in the most enlightened and ancient of times."

All quoted poetry is from The Selected Poems of T'ao Ch'ien, *translated by David Hinton, Copper Canyon Press, 1993.*

Psychotropics
A Quick Hit from an Interglacial Age

After the Glaciers

IN THE WANING YEARS of the last century, the view we homo sapiens hold of our species changed considerably. One shift, which may take a while to settle into the collective mind, came through the discovery of two remarkable caves in southern France filled with Ice Age murals. For scientists, artists, and historians, what was found in these limestone caverns pushed back the horizons on human image making to an unexpected distance. What were our ancestors up to in those deep stretches of time during the last glaciation? ("I know what happened before the after and after the before," says Coyote Old Man rather darkly in Jaime de Angulo's *Indian Tales.*)

First came discovery in 1991, under dramatic circumstances, of Paleolithic art in the Cosquer Cave on the Mediterranean coast near the French city of Marseilles. The cave entrance lies in a cliff wall a hundred and twenty feet below the water's surface. To get into the spacious, calcite encrusted cavern where the art lies, divers had to swim nearly five hundred feet through a narrow passage. Inside the cave, preserved by coatings of calcite and long steady temperatures (since the retreat of the glaciers the entrance has been sealed by water), they found a profusion of animal images. Many were already known from other caves in France and Spain: horse, bison, ibex, chamois, red deer, the now extinct giant elk, and a cat head. There are also eight seals, three auk (a seabird, like a thick penguin, hunted to extinction in the nineteenth century), one fish, and some odd creatures that look like jellyfish. No sea creature had been previously encountered in Paleolithic cave art.

Then, in mid-December 1994, some professional spelunkers and cave art enthusiasts entered a little crack in the karstic rock at the base of a high cliff in the Ardèche region of France. They squirmed headfirst through a rabbit hole and nearly tumbled straight down into an enormous cavern. Lowering themselves fifty feet with the help of a ladder, they found in a sequence of "galleries" a trove of old art—approximately three hundred animal figures, and hundreds of abstract "signs." The principal creatures depicted established an entirely different pantheon or iconography for cave art than had been previously encountered, both through the dominance of certain animals and the uniqueness of others. The most featured animals are the maneless cave lion, cave bear, giant elk, and woolly mammoth. There are also a spotted panther, an owl, and a possible hyena, none of which had been seen before. Equally dramatic is the vast litter of cave bear bones. One bear skull has invited much speculation because it had been set on a rock in the center of one deep chamber.

The artists of this cave, now called Chauvet after one of its discoverers, seem the equal in confidence and technique of any Japanese Zen brush-stroke artist or abstractionist of modern America. An unexcelled vitality emanates from the large murals of bovines, lions and horses. Radiocarbon dating of charcoal used in the black lines of the paintings proves the art to be nearly 31,000 years old—nearly twice as distant from us in time as the images drawn at Lascaux.

Chronologically, the final example of Pleistocene cave art found in that part of the world, at Le Portel in the Ariège, dates at just over 11,000 years. This brings the art form down to the inception of the Holocene and the worldwide retreat of the glaciers. Upper Paleolithic cave art was a tradition that lasted twenty thousand years.

At this juncture in history, if one is to adhere to—say, *inhabit*—a myth—or in the widest sense, a religion—and to find a way past the distressing fractiousness of twentieth century ideologies—such a mythos would have to accommodate a scope of this sort. Archaeological time, and behind that geological time, setting the context. What spadework, paleontology, and computer reconstruction uncover are the elements of a deep puzzle. Now—what are we to *make* of the fossil record? Putting it in these terms reminds me of the lovely conceit that humans learnt writing by observing bird tracks left on the sand.

There has been an undercurrent of speculation that cave artists from the Aurignacian through the Magdalenian periods were possibly jazzed on some psychedelic. Poet and long-time scholar of Paleolithic art Clayton Eshleman alerted me to this in conversation a number of years ago. It's a proposition that will probably never go away since it is unlikely ever to be proven or discredited—though one can't discount the possibility of new discoveries or emergent scientific methods able to read further details into the archaeological traces left by Paleolithic master painters.

I have not logged a great deal of time in the caves. In 1982 I got into Font-de-Gauma and a few minor caves for a tour during the off-season. What I remember best is the palpably breathing quality of the caves, layered with glistening calcaceous deposits of subtle color—as though they were alive—and of course the three dimensional fore-quarters of the horse in Font-de-Gauma, conceived by its artist around a mineral outcropping. My intuition from that vivid trip—if you need to push the question of humans employing specific methods to alter their minds—is that time spent in the caves themselves could be sufficient.

Stretches of time under the mineral earth, where no light gets in except what was brought by the artists themselves, would bring all manner of vivid synaesthetic turns to thought and sensation. The splendidly conceived paintings, thundering with *ch'i*, were often set deliberately far back from cave entrances, high on walls or ceilings, inside chimneys, or deep within hard to reach galleries. At that depth torches provide a startling luminous dance among colorful soapy stalagmites and glistening calcite crust. Recovered artifacts show that in some caves the artists used tiny terracotta lamps balanced on scaffolds. Modern diggers found dozens of such lamps in Lascaux, each so small it could only have illuminated a fragment of one of the great painted panels. Engaging theories put forward, first by the Abbé Breuil, then by André Leroi-Gourhan, are unconvincing as to what the paintings meant or what they might have been used for. Clayton Eshleman has visited and revisited the caves and logged many hours in them. He writes a poetry unique in its image and syntax, and aligns it to what he calls a tradition of "the grotesque," emphasizing the etymological origin of the word: "of the grottoes."

What is the current anthropological and ethnobotanical view on the use of psychoactive substances among archaic peoples? A burgeoning field with many distinguished scholars today—not at all a crackpot area of study—so much material has come to light it is nearly impossible to keep up with. Particularly if you bring in the psychologists, theorists, the brilliant sometimes cranky popularists. I've always cottoned to Weston LaBarre's careful look at religion's possible origins in the use of psychoactive plants. (Current ethnobotanist friends prefer the term *entheogen*, a neologism drawn from classical Greek by R. Gordon Wasson and used by his colleagues, which holds the rough meaning "inner divinity," or colloquially "waking the god within"). The question seems to stand like this: do the origins of religion and art lie largely in the use of mind altering substances? Sometimes?

Not at all? Mircea Eliade, author of the groundbreaking *Shamanism: Archaic Techniques of Ecstasy*, insisted that use of plant substances to reach "beyond the pale" was historically a late development. He believed utilization of psychotropics as a visionary technique showed Asiatic shamanism (the prototype from which he drew) in decline or decadence. There is testimony however that near the end of his life he modified his views. A profusion of evidence with regard to both the centrality and antiquity of the use of plant substances had started to come in from ethnographers working in Mexico and Central and South America.

LaBarre's starting point, though, is a problematic riddle for ethnobotanists: why the extensive and well documented use of entheogens in the New World—tobacco, ayahuasca, peyote, mescal buttons, psilocybin mushrooms, and dozens of other barks, leafs, roots, fruit? By comparison why has there been found so little entheogenic use in the Old? The Old World—Asia, Europe, Africa—has always had larger hominid populations, more numerous and diversified cultures, and probably more plant species. What would account for the enormous pharmacology of mind-altering substances among Western Hemisphere residents, yet a relatively empty medicine cabinet once you cross Beringia or the Pacific Ocean and return to Asia?

Worth noting here: there is not consensus on how long the New World has been populated. A standard timeline of about 12,000 years accords with the most recent glaciation and a tundra land-bridge between Siberia and Alaska. This was the Würm period, when the climate was harsh and current sea levels might have been lower by as much as four hundred feet, permitting land migration across an unbroken stretch of the Bering Strait, possibly sixty-two miles wide at that point. There are archaeological findings throughout the Americas, however, which defy this timeline, pushing it much farther back into the past. Some Native American scholars question the entire model of New World populations arriving from elsewhere, "on the hoof" along with herds of large game from Asia.

It is LaBarre's surmise, though, that Paleolithic gatherer/hunters who migrated across Beringia during the last glaciation (along with the mastodon, a small horse, and the dire wolf) would have been "culturally programmed for an interest in hallucinogens." Pan-Asiatic shamanism, he speculates, rooted in the Pleistocene period, with its intense premium placed on individual, existential vision, is the religious attitude or *complex* the pioneers would have carried. Notable here are that some of these complexes are still extant in stretches of Siberia, and have started to vigorusly reassert themselves after the collapse of the Soviet Union. Rather than a tribe unified by common ritual, the concerns of myth, healing, and religion would have fallen into the hands of anarchic vision specialists, alert to assistance from allies in the natural world. They would have been on the lookout wherever they traveled for psychotropic plant or animal products.

This stands in contrast to the priesthood, sacrificial surplus, and well defined hierarchies—organized religion—of Neolithic planting cultures. Peter Lamborn Wilson comments, "We might say that shamanic hunters use hallucinogens to structure individual relations with spirits, while agriculturists tend toward greater ritualization and socialization of entheogenic experience."

New World nomad pioneer settlers, LaBarre speculates, brought an active interest in psychotropic plants from a *then similarly obsessed* Old World; which Old World eventually underwent so-called agricultural "revolution" much earlier and far more extensively than did any reach of the New. Use of psychotropics for visionary purposes would have been increasingly ritualized and socialized in Asia and Europe, carefully regulated, possibly taxed, and finally eliminated by emergent castes of priests. This he thinks wiped out predilection throughout much of Asia towards psychotropic plant ingestion. And left the New World, in LaBarre's phrase, "ethnographically a kind of Paleo-Mesolithic *fossil* of the Old World."

It's right here I get most caught on the cultures of South Asia. These particular Old World complexes never came away from that shamanic edge. Despite settling into agriculture possibly more than ten millennia back, despite the loss sometime in the second millennium BCE of the identity of Soma (evidently a potent psychotropic medicine that defines Vedic culture), the tilt towards personal vision *stayed*. It shows up in India's philosophy, folklore, song, and poetry right down to contemporary times. Wendy Doniger, a fine, insightful, and exuberant scholar of Sanskrit, has remarked that you can understand almost all of subsequent Indian culture activity—art, yoga, tantra, ritual—as an attempt to recover the early Soma experience.

A first good icon for India: the Mohenjo Daro clay seal imprinted with an antlered cross-legged figure. Eyes closed, cock erect, he sits surrounded by megafauna that hold an intriguing species connection to those depicted in the caves of South France and northern Spain. Tiger, elephant, rhinoceros, goat—and a bovine that more resembles the extinct auroch of European cave paintings than any bull or buffalo I've seen traveling around contemporary India. This little clay-print image, its blend of human and animal features instantly recalling the mongrel "sorcerer" of Les Trois Frères in the French Pyrenees, has been dated at 3000-2000 BCE. Weirdly, in India he seems right up to date.

People looking pointedly like that clay image wander the length and breadth of India to this day. The generic term is *sādhu*: seeker of verities. A Sanskrit word, it means one who goes right to the goal, spiritual liberation, bypassing all social obligations. Originally it's a term used in archery: hitting the bull's eye. Formally outcaste, but unquestionably located at India's psychic and social center, the fiercely individualistic sādhu serves as a living reminder throughout South Asia of all the things poetry and religion keep talking about. That's why sādhus manage to subsist on alms. Who knows where they've been traveling? Matted dreadlocks caked with cow dung and crematory ash. Deliberately nameless, dressed in a robe (the usual color is saffron, thought to derive from archaic ocher, the color of life, though occasionally you see scarier wanderers clad in black robes). They carry a begging bowl (the most frightful ones will utilize a human skull for an eating bowl). Young Indians and Westerners seek them out for spiritual counsel and the enormously good ganja and bhang to which they have access. Some carry the iron trident of Śiva Paśupati, Lord of Beasts, who is variously shown with an attendant bull, a tiger skin, seated crosslegged, ithyphallic, and possibly horned—like that clay image from Mohenjo Daro.

The trident, says Eliade, was an instrument common to the Eurasian shaman.

Soma

India developed the most sustained post-psychedelic civilization on earth.

Approximately 3700 years ago the Indo-European invaders who took over North India organized the oral poems of the *Ṛg Veda* into *maṇḍalas*, or cycles. Translators use the term "books" but that is a late inference—the poems surely existed orally, "on the tongue," for as long as they have been known in written form. Similarly, the Vedic terms for individual poems are *stuti* and *stotra*. Both refer to a poem that's sung, not to a didactic text recited. Western scholars persist in calling them hymns, Greek for praise song—accurate enough—except for how the word carries in Protestant cultures a rather strong whiff of piety. Among the Vedic *stotra* are a surprising tribute to gamblers, one to frogs, and one to a mysterious female guardian of the forests, Āraṇyakī.

The stotra of the Veda, probably in circulation in various rhythmic and musical forms long before being collected into sequences, came to be the property of specific clans and are mostly addressed to divinities. They remain central to various sacrificial rituals by Brahmin priests. A large number address a deity called Soma, who in fact gets more poems than any other of the Vedic gods. Soma was identified with the moon, with a specific plant, with a beverage made from that plant, and possibly a particular state of mind. By 1700 BCE Soma was the milk of existence—a drink, a plant, a god, the moon—a mysterious liquid concocted on Earth from an herb or root, a leaf or mushroom that no modern Vedic scholar or ethnobotanist has convincingly identified. From the Soma plant came a beverage, an elaborately brewed decoction, drunk by the Indo-European horse-and-chariot nomads who coming out of Central Asia had settled east of the Indus River. One theory, developed by R. Gordon Wasson, holds that they fed it to their steeds and drank the urine, letting the animal kidney filter out unpleasant alkaloids.

Poet priests ingested the drink during the Vedic rituals, and by all accounts received a powerful psychotropic effect. It made them feel like gods, omniscient, riding the winds, able to move the planet at will. Among other effects it provided a state of consciousness that gave access to the poems of the *Rg Veda*. Once taken, Soma clearly transfigured the drinker into a divinely inspired singer. Yet composing and arranging into cycles the so-called hymns of the *Rg Veda* they claim they merely took what they heard, poems already existent. I'm put in mind of Ezra Pound's lovely phrase: "gathered from the air a live tradition." Soma made them the gift. It's unclear whether they saw or heard the poems—probably both at once—which are qualified as *apaurusheya*, not of human origin. What resulted anyhow was something that seems to occur worldwide with shamans: the visionary goes out of his or her head and comes back with a song.

> This, yes, this is my thought: I will win a cow and a horse.
>> Have I not drunk Soma?
> Like impetuous winds, the drinks have lifted me up.
>> Have I not drunk Soma?
> The drinks have lifted me up, like swift horses bolting with a chariot.
>> Have I not drunk Soma?
> The prayer has come to me as a lowing cow comes to her beloved son.
>> Have I not drunk Soma?
> I turn the prayer around in my heart, as a wheelwright turns a
> chariot seat.
>> Have I not drunk Soma?

. . . .

In my vastness, I surpassed the sky and this vast earth.
    Have I not drunk Soma?
Yes! I will place the earth here, or perhaps there.
    Have I not drunk Soma?

(translation from *Ṛg Veda* 10.119 by Wendy Doniger O'Flaherty)

About 3000 years ago Soma vanished from use (source dried up; or lit-eralist priests led an inquisition against high-spirited poets; or somebody held the secret too tight and forgot to impart it before dying—nobody knows). It had been for the cognoscenti the potent instigator of poetic vi-sion, a forceful psychedelic prepared and ingested in a ritual setting, that resulted in wordcraft.

To this day Brahmin priests perform the Soma ritual, though every-one involved admits that the original identity of Soma has been lost for a long time. The common modern substitue for Soma in Brahmin ritual is *Ephedra*, which gives a slight buzz. Sir William Jones, early British San-skrit scholar thought it might be wild rue. Others thought alcohol, which it couldn't have been. The description of its preparation rules out fermentation.

In 1968 Gordon Wasson published *Soma: Divine Mushroom of Immortal-ity*, the first attempt to bring together textual studies with the findings of ethnobotany. He identified the plant of the *Ṛg Veda* with *Amanita muscaria,* the fly agaric mushroom, which has been regularly used in temperate zones as a psychoactive. Fly agaric is still in use today in Siberia—the Santa Claus mushroom with the white stalk, scarlet cap, and white spots or flecks, which still figures in Eastern European folk art.

Haoma and Harmaline, by D.S. Flattery and Martin Schwartz (1989), was an important cross-cultural effort to get at the old question of what plant soma was. The authors go to Iranian sources, from the *Gāthās* of Zarathustra to contemporary folk medicine. They provide a convincing al-ternative to Wasson's *tour de force* stab at identity. Flattery and Schwartz's proposal: that Iranian *haoma* (Vedic *soma*) was *Perganum harmala*, harmel or wild rue. *Not* Wasson's fly agaric, which he, Wasson, copped from Siberia and his earlier mushroom studies in Russia, and seemed predisposed to find in India once he got on the track.

Soma's identity remains an intriguing mystery for ethnobotanists, Vedic scholars, and interested experimenters with entheogens, but there's another issue at stake. How necessary was it for the poetry? Even in the West the importance of psychoactive substances for poetry, at least for the production of some of it, can't be ignored. There's Coleridge's opium visions, the widespread use of absinthe in France, Balzac's toxic quantities of caffeine, and Rimbaud's call to arms for the poet to systematically derange the senses through drugs and other means. I've always suspected these to be better thought of as mythic accounts or anti-bourgeois manifestos than actual necessities to the poetry. This seems more the spirit of the Surrealists and renegades like René Daumal. I find very little good poetry of recent decades—even of the psychedelic sixties—that has come explicitly out of hallucinogenic trips.

Peter Lamborn Wilson, in a good contemporary survey of possible Celtic and Irish connections to Soma, introduces the phrase "Soma-function": a kind of archetypal experience important in its mythological structure but not reliant on any particular substance.

After Wasson, we can no longer read certain ancient texts without the psychedelic hypothesis—that is, without assuming the existence of efficacious entheogenic sacraments in many world cultures. If Wasson can be faulted, it is perhaps for his over-precise identification of certain sacraments with mushrooms. He was a mycologist, after all, and he had his prejudices. He paid little attention to non-fungal hallucinogens, but the plant world suffers an embarrassment of riches when it comes to psychotropic substances, and mushrooms have no monopoly. Even if Amanita muscaria can be accepted as the "original" Soma, any entheogenic substance can be "substituted" for another: they are symbolically identical because equally efficacious. The important result of Wasson's work concerns not so much the identity of Soma as it concerns the "Soma-function," the ecstatic transformation of ordinary consciousness by an ingested psychotropic substance.

Around 1992, before Harry Smith's important *Anthology of American Folk Music* got reprinted bringing him mild posthumous fame, Harry lived in a little cottage on the grounds of The Naropa Institute, mostly off money provided by the Grateful Dead. People spoke of him as the place's resident shaman, and he did seem to know quite a bit about psychedelics from a lifetime of off-the-track trips, delving into art, anthropology, linguistics, film, the occult. There circulated all manner of story about his range of beyond the pale activities. In the days he lived at Naropa it was standard to stop by his cottage on the way across campus—for a quick smoke of good marijuana and some sharp conversation on practically any topic you wanted. A summer day in 1992, over some smoke, I asked what he thought Soma was. Wild rue like Sanskrit scholars David Flattery and Martin Schwartz suggest? *Amanita muscaria,* as Wasson claimed? Some other hidden South Asian vine or root or bud?

Taking a quick hit, Harry fiddled with the portable tape recorder he always carried (he was collecting material for Dada type cut-ups of human noise patterns). "Wasson is full of shit."

A Taste for Old Poems

Nobody who has looked at the evidence any longer believes that use of psychedelic substances simply indicates a culture in decline. Spiritual traditions reliant on complex preparation of psychedelics, and formed around the visions and insights delivered, are firmly established by anthropologists on every continent. They clearly go back into deep history. So, from the other side: are the renegade futurist scholars right, that those who *don't* use mind-altering medicines are a group of boring anti-evolutionist squares?

"The self-nature of poetry is rasa," wrote a fourteenth century yogin and poet from India, Viśvanātha, in his composition handbook the *Sahitya-darpana* or *Mirror of Writing*. Rasa has been the key term in Indian art, especially poetry and theater, since the first archaic instruction book appeared, the *Nātya Śāstra*. To my mind rasa is a transparent substitute for Soma, but an enormously effective one. The word first meant sap, juice, nectar, semen, fluid. It was the liquid precipitate of anything, the circulatory fluid vital to a living body or system—spirit juice. By extension it came to mean "taste, flavor, seasoning," as in "the wild game flavor;" more abstractly, it meant essence.

In art rasa means the emotional territory or moods worked by a poem, piece of music, dance, or dramatic performance. There's no word in American English that adequately gets at it. The French poet René Daumal (1908-1944), about the only modern Western artist to deeply study the traditions of Indian poetics and learn Sanskrit, translated it into French as *saveur,* a word cognate to English savor. But savor doesn't come across with much kick in our wide ranging American patois.

The intriguing thing about rasa is that its constellation of ideas, which rose in India a thousand years or more after the identity of Soma had disappeared, seems to be modeled on Soma—or on Peter Wilson's Soma-function—but gets to it in a topsy-turvy manner. It inverts cause and effect. If for Vedic seers Soma was the drink, thus the ritually prepared substance that altered consciousness and instigated poetry, rasa is its opposite, the result not the origin of ceremonial poetry. The point of devising a poem is to use all the complex layers of language in order to produce the juice, the taste of a primordial experience. Not a vague mood or transitory passion like emotions in every day life, which rise, disappear, imperfectly manifest, get mixed, are unstable; instead, something felt with utter archaic clarity: a transformed state of being.

John Cage called rasa a "permanent emotion." It would be the direct and non-paraphrasable taste of primordial experience. So immediate is its impact (everyone knows but no one can really explain how art provokes actual physical changes in the body, like bristling hair or skin, abrupt weeping, or eyesight brought to unprecedented clarity) that poets in India likened it to taste; taste being the only sense in which to perceive you have to actually take something into your body. The old yogins regarded taste as primordial, more basic than touch or sight. In the eighth century Vidyā had noted rasa's effect in a poem:

I praise that silent
listener
her whole body bristling—
only a poet
linking words with ineluctable cadence
can touch
her entrails with fire.

Poetry became the old ritual sacrifice, pressing out of nothing but words and their rhythms the psychotropic (spirit-altering) juice. Maybe it finds a way to reach into language's remote and archaic origins, to that grotto where language and the world still seem joined. This separates it from ordinary speech or writing. Poetry—literature, song—does not lose its value once the words have been heard. Could this be because its words do not seem to be about something, but *are the thing itself?*

The Indian tradition distinguishes eight rasas, naming them after the everyday emotions they resemble. And centuries before Rimbaud gave colors to vowels, the poets of old India with their psychedelic delight in lists and associations ascribed to the elements of language a whole range of correspondences: colors, seasons, plants, animals, musical scales, cycles of history, particular deities. Books on poetry were actually grimoires of culture and ecology, whole grammars of the planet's elements and how they corresponded to speech-sounds.

Here is a list of the rasas, their Sanskrit terms and associated colors:

The Eight Rasas	Sanskrit Term	Color
Erotic	*sṛngāra*	lustrous black, raven
Comic	*hāsya*	white
Grievous	*karuṇa*	light gray
Angry	*raudra*	red
Heroic	*vīra*	skin color, pale green
Fearsome	*bhayānaka*	charcoal black
Odious	*bībhatsa*	blue
Marvelous	*adbhuta*	yellow

Srṅgāra, the erotic rasa, was considered the most important, which is why Sanskrit poetry produced an enormous number of exquisite, compressed love lyrics. Love would be the sentient body's original language, closest to the truth of things. This very simply explains the erotic sculpture that adorns so many of India's temples, the hallucinatory range of love depicted: heterosexual, homosexual, inventive group sex, sex among animals, sex in virtually every imaginable posture. The erotic also has one very unusual quality—it covers two different emotional tones: love-in-enjoyment, and love-in-separation.

To the above list some add a ninth rasa: *śanta,* the spiritually tranquil.

Each rasa has its particular powers: in music it is the rāga, the scale or particular notes and progressions; in poetry or drama they are the specific articulate sounds, the metric structures, the durations. To provoke a rasa, the arts used a brilliant synaesthesia. Training in poetry, as in all the arts, would have been a yogic discipline that included years of meditation on the associations of sound, color, elements of ecology, and so forth. (The Indian poets said that to be a "person with heart" or a skilled auditor of poetry and thus prepared to experience the consciousness opening effect of rasa, you had to put yourself through training as deliberate as the artist.) Rimbaud envisioned a poem that could be a blazing light show or dance of colors. India imagined the same thing; but seasons, plants, animals, historical events, and deities danced among the vowels and consonants as well.

All this was meant to induce a completely altered consciousness, a state of spiritual wakening. The critics called rasa the "twin sister of samādhi," that state of absorbed wakefulness Lama Govinda believed was first cultivated by Paleolithic hunters in the Himalayan foothills. Some handbooks made claims for rasa that sound strikingly close to what the Vedic poet, ceremonially lit up by Soma, had described two thousand years earlier. Compare this philosophic verse by Ānandavardhana (ninth century Kashmir) with the Vedic poem quoted above.

> In the boundless realm of poetry
> the poet is the sole creator.
> Things are transformed

at his pleasure.
If the poet wakens love in his poem
all things are suffused with rasa—
if he lacks passion, nothing has rasa.
Mastering the elements,
a skilled poet makes inert things sentient,
sentient creatures inert—
all he desires comes into existence.

BIBLIOGRAPHY

Ānandavardhana. *Dhvanyāloka:Text with English Translation and Notes.*
K. Krishnamoorthy. Motilal Banarsidass: Delhi, 1974.

Chauvet, Jean-Marie et. al. *Dawn of Art:The Chauvet Cave.* Abrams: New York, 1996.

Clottes, Jean and Jean Courtin. *The Cave Beneath the Sea: Paleolithic Images at Cosquer.*
Abrams: New York, 1996.

Daumal, René. *Rasa: Or Knowledge of the Self.* Trans. Louise Landes Levi.
New Directions: New York, 1982.

Eliade, Mircea. *Shamanism:Archaic Techniques of Ecstasy.* Princeton University Press:
Princeton, 1964.

Flattery, David and Martin Schwartz. *Haoma and Harmoline:The Botanical Identity
of the Indo-Iranian Sacred Hallucinogen "Haoma" and Its Legacy in Religion, Language
and Middle Eastern Folklore.* University of California Publications in Near Eastern
Studies v. 21. Berkeley, 1989.

Ingalls, Daniel, and Jeffrey Masson and M.V. Patwardahn. *The Dhvanyāloka of
Ānandavardhana with the Locana of Abhinavagupta.* Harvard Oriental Series 49.
Harvard University Press: Cambridge, 1990.

La Barre, Weston. "Hallucinogens and the Shamanic Origins of Culture" in Peter Furst, *Flesh of the Gods*. Praeger: New York, 1972.

O'Flaherty, Wendy Doniger. *The Rig Veda*. Penguin Books: New York, 1981.

Viśvanātha Kaviraja. *Sahitya-Darpaṇa*. Annotated with Introduction and Explanatory Notes by Pandit Durgaprasāda Dvideva. Nirnāya Sāgara Press: Bombay, 1936.

Wasson, R. Gordon. *Soma: Divine Mushroom of Immortality*. Harcourt, Brace and World: New York, 1968.

Wilson, Peter Lamborn. *Ploughing the Clouds: The Search for Irish Soma*. City Lights: San Francisco, 1999.

Questionnaire

First Facts

What animal before being born human?

What plant?

Tallest mountain attempted? The most treacherous?

How were you nearly killed by the residents of a far-off nation?

Three books you'd take to the woods.

Getting in Deeper

Intentional community (utopian, anarchist, feminist, archaic)
you might have lived in before it was scattered by officers of the State.

Historical epoch suited best to your temper. Give three lines from
a poem you composed there.

Writer prior to the 20th century you would most like to sleep with.

Most useful oracle.

Dictionary most frequently visited.

These are the "permanent emotions" (India): erotic, comic,
compassionate, angry, heroic, fearsome, odious, marvelous, tranquil.
Add two more, including one known only to yourself.

Foreign language you have vowed to master this lifetime.

Melville, Thoreau, Dickinson, Whitman, or Sor Juana Inés de la Cruz?
Anne Bradstreet, Frederick Douglas, Chief Joseph, Mother Jones?

The Rites of Night & Day

Pencil, pen, typewriter, laptop, or pocket knife?

Philosopher never read, but instinctively know has altered your life.

On a rocky outcropping, in a car, in a cafe, gone "virtual,"
or sequestered among books?

Skills mastered in sleep.

Power objects you carry or wear at all times. Some of the time. To bed.

Magdalena, Odulvai, Tun Huang, or Hovenweep?

Who among the old gods and goddesses?

Farther back?

Pilgrimage to Buddhist India

"THE HOUSEHOLDER'S LIFE," says old Buddha's document *The Dīgha Nikkāya,* "is full of dust and hindrance." And immediately you feel it, right in your shoes. From its beginnings, Buddhism has shown a sharp impatience for stay-at-home habits. It has spread out from India, traveled to China and Japan, braved the mountains into Tibet, gone to Southeast Asia, Europe and America, and in twenty-five hundred years hasn't shaken that fine old scepticism.

The impulse to ramble is as old as humankind. We have ample testimony of a close ancestral connection to migratory animals, and it appears that the earliest calendars were incised animal bone, small enough to slip in a pocket as the human clan arranged its year by traveling to seasonal food sources. Archaeologists are uncovering routes of migration our human forebears followed, keeping herds of reindeer and antelope, bison and sheep in sight. For most human beings, for tens of thousands of years, home was quite literally "on the hoof." The hunter, the nomad, the rambler, and finally the pilgrim. Perhaps it is no more than the swift human intellect and our proud, strong legs pursuing a primordial hunger to see what's around the bend, over the next hill, or just upriver.

Every child grows up on a landscape both seen and imagined. Parents, relatives, and friends bring home tales of marvelous places. The elderly revisit their childhood landscapes by turning them into deeply revealing stories. These brilliant outward-looking eyes never quite catch up with that shimmering ability to see things and locations within. Poems, journals, hagiographies, the diaries of merchants and seekers, accounts of sailors and soldiers—traditions of storytelling never disappear. How many records do the libraries hold now of visits to India—a continent known in its own treasury of tale and legend as Jambudvīpa, the Rose-Apple Island?

Tale and legend? Stations of pilgrimage, like stories, get more, not less rich as the generations roll past. The earliest human art—cliff walls pecked with meaningful designs or pictographs—caves delicately and inspiration-ally peopled with ocher and manganese animal forms—were not under-taken at places of permanent residence. These were locales to which people journeyed, passing along them on migratory circuits, or at a later date making special efforts to visit: they were ceremonial centers, shrines, locations of brave human deeds and brilliant supernatural events. Peerless art and innovative architecture arise to commemorate the old stories, and in their wake spring up field tents, kitchens, inns, or little guest lodges, to make the sites hospitable for visitors. Everyone hungers to visit and revisit the locales associated with legend. To some, this life of rambling and migra-tion takes such hold of the imagination that it comes to seem the one life worth leading—if only for some brief period. If only once in a lifetime.

The early Buddhists were an order of wandering alms-seekers. A rag-tag bunch, they could be found at crossroads and river fords, along high-ways, camping in city parks, or sheltering in forest groves. India would scarcely offer such a range of destinations for the Buddhist pilgrim had Shakyamuni Buddha settled into a secluded ashram like the Brahmin priests of his period, or lived out his days as a philosopher king in his father's pal-ace. The model he took for himself and his followers—that of philosophical rambler, beggar of food, tatter-robed paraclete, inveterate pilgrim—was an old one. For centuries before his birth others had gone to the forests and highways, tired of rigid social forms and a predictable religion of the kitchen and bedroom. India's great casteless community of the homeless was already ancient in Buddha's day.

The pilgrim, the wanderer, the forest-dweller: figures so familiar to the old epics, to poetry and legend, that the arts of India seem thronged with them. The Buddha's resolve as a young man to leave his father's pal-ace, what the annals call his Great Going-Forth, came after seeing the Four Signs. On successive days he encountered an old man, a sick man, a corpse, and lastly, a wandering mendicant on perpetual pilgrimage to the source of life. You meet similar mendicants on every pilgrimage route in India today, at all the temples and riverbanks. You see them on trains, in taxis and rickshaws, traveling by private cars. But mostly they have gone and continue to go forth by foot.

How can we separate the notion of pilgrimage from that primal impulse to set out on a walk, shake off the householder's dust, and simply see something new? Our bones ache with it. The word *pilgrim* along with its Latin original, *peregrine*, simply means a person who wanders "across the land." Old Sanskrit words from India which refer to the pilgrim spring from the same irresistible source. A *yātrika* is a rambler, a *tīrthayātrika* a wanderer who frequents crossroads and riverbanks. You may think the world of nation states, superhighways, and rigidly drawn borders no longer accomodates such folk, but in India they ramble as they have for millennia—a tradition that traces itself back to a prehistoric pan-Asiatic shamanism. Today's sādhu, clutching a trident or carrying the mark of the trident drawn in ash on his forehead, carries one of the oldest paraphernalia of the Asiatic shaman.

It was near Taxila in 323 BC, after fording the Indus River, that Alexander the Great's army encountered a community of spiritual goers-forth. The fierce, ragged, skull-carrying mendicants they met were not Buddhists but Hindu sādhus—on pilgrimage into Himalayan foothills holy to Śiva. But before the Greek soldiers were done with India they would bring back accounts of a Buddhist civilization that took for its principal emblem the *śramaṇa* or homeless wanderer, who owned only a patchwork robe, a needle to mend it, a begging bowl, and a razor to tonsure the head. The Greeks coined their own term, *gymnosophist*—naked philosopher—to describe these figures. And ever since, homeless men and women of religion, perpetual pilgrims, have exerted the strongest fascination over foreign travelers to India—probably because nowhere else has such a community so durably established itself. Buddhism picked the archaic tradition up from epic and folklore and placed the wanderer at the core of its discipline.

Even the initial settling in of the *bhikku* and *bhikkunī* (ordained monk and nun), which occurred during Buddha's lifetime, did not spell an end to the wandering life. It arose as a provisional response to cycles of weather. July and August are India's monsoon season. Every year torrential rains pour from the sky, rivers overflow, and water makes the roads nearly impassable. Shakyamuni Buddha counseled his students to sit out the periodic downfalls at specified rain-retreats. Certain of these shelters developed over time into permanent way stations. Some received donations of land and used financial gifts to raise walls and spires, meditation halls, stūpas and libraries. With the blossoming of Buddhist civilization, the vast *vihāras* of north India evolved from these periodic way stations: centers of meditation, art, learning, philosophical debate, and trade. The one at Nalanda, founded in the fourth century in the present-day state of Bihar, accommodated up to ten thousand resident yogins, scholars, tradesmen, and artists at a time. Yet for all the massive walls, the kitchens and libraries, the halls of worship, no concept of staying put ever fully caught on. Etymologically, the word *vihāra* means "a place to wander about." To consider these way stations colleges or monasteries misses something crucial. You'll see, if you visit the expansive courtyards and long sheltered arcades of Nalanda, that its residents thought the best seeking and most subtly colored thinking was still to be done on foot.

What is this thinking done on foot? Ask any pilgrim, you'll get the same answer: You only find out by going. It is an attitude towards life, not a catechism had from some book. Old Buddha ancestor of North America, Henry David Thoreau, gets as close as anyone has to writing it down. In his essay "Walking" he tracks the word *saunter* to Old French *Sainte Terre*—holy land. A saunterer is a holy-lander, a walker to sacred places and storied locations. "We should," he admonishes, "go forth on the shortest walk, perchance, in the spirit of undying adventure, never to return—prepared to send back our embalmed hearts only as relics to our desolate kingdoms." It's here he gives a taste of that adventurous urge which forms the pilgrim's resolve. "If you are ready to leave father and mother, brother and sister, and wife and child and friends, and never see them again,—if you have paid your debts, and made your will, and settled all your affairs, and are a free man, then you are ready for a walk."

Only the walker who sets out towards ultimate things is a pilgrim. In this lies the terrible difference between tourist and pilgrim. The tourist travels just as far, sometimes with great zeal and courage, gathering up acquisitions (a string of adventures, a wondrous tale or two) and returns the same person as the one who departed. There is something inexpressibly sad in the clutter of belongings the tourist unpacks back at home.

The pilgrim is different. The pilgrim resolves that the one who returns will not be the same person as the one who set out. Pilgrimage is a passage for the reckless and subtle. The pilgrim—and the metaphor comes to us from distant times—must be prepared to shed the husk of personality or even the body like a worn out coat. A Buddhist dictum has it that "the Way exists but not the traveler on it." And when you peruse the journals, books, and poems left behind by travelers of the Buddhist world—to India, to China or Japan, to Tibet—you find a curious insight. For the pilgrim the road is home; reaching your destination seems nearly inconsequential.

No pilgrim to Buddhist India has left more compelling an account than seventh-century Chinese monk Hsüan-tsang. I'd call him the patron saint of the pilgrim. His own record of the twenty-year journey describes in vivid terms the elemental recklessness you need if you would become a pilgrim. You must be as much rogue as saint, as much buccaneer as contemplative. Simply to get out of T'ang Dynasty China, Hsüan-tsang had to break an imperial decree, bribe a series of border guards, and slip off towards barbarian lands in disguise. And that was the easy part. From there his way was beset by bandits, fierce desert storms, unscalable mountains, savage beasts. Fearsome supernatural creatures would lurk at every turn of the road, but over the border he goes like a convict over the wall, and never looks back. Wu Ch'eng-En's delightful book, *Journey to the West,* or in Arthur Waley's translation, *Monkey,* provides Hsüan-tsang with a rascally, trickster monkey for alter ego and guardian, giving the tale a fabulous coloring: pilgrim and irrepressibly mischievous monkey, bound to each other as they pursue a supernatural journey into old India. Everyone heading off to the Buddhist sites of India should read it. For on that vast subcontinent, your own mind, so similar to the silly, aggressive rhesus monkeys you meet every day on the roads of South Asia, will be your greatest nemesis. That same mind is also your only protector.

What I mean is that excessive piety does not prove particularly useful to the Buddhist practitioner. What an impediment it is to the pilgrim! If your temperament impels you towards the sites of the Buddhist world, especially those spread across the Gangetic Plain, you're going to need to be loose, spontaneous, charitable, open-eyed, humorous, unsentimental as you encounter India's endless string of beggars, cripples, lepers, dirty children, imploring mothers, avaricious merchants. You need generosity but not lavishness, determination but not rigidity. You need a dry wit, even a trace of irreverence. These help the inner organs, assist the appetite, and certainly make more tolerable Bodh Gaya's scorching winds or those aggressive flies in the teashops of Lucknow.

Chuckling demons are likely to strew your path with impediments. If you take the pilgrim's route to India, you must be prepared for nearly anything—for misguided companions, bad food, crowded trains, for pickpockets, unreliable buses, filthy toilets. And most of all, for that endlessly irritating monkey companion: your own peevish egoism.

Going to India in 1992, my third trip, I expected to visit the Buddhist sites of the north. Some I'd not seen in twenty years, some not at all. Bodh Gaya, Sarnath, Nalanda, Lumbini…. I intended to bow my head at each. But in Calcutta my companion and I found our plane tickets no good—the airlines on strike. No one had warned us. Refugees from religious riots that were flaring in Bombay and Lucknow choked all the trains. Even a taxi could not get over the bridges that might lead us west. We raged and worried, we raced about town. But through some baffling string of events we landed on a train winding south, and in a few days found ourselves outside Bhubaneshwar, from which Buddhism had been brutally driven twelve hundred years earlier. On a massive rock overlooking the field where Buddhist king Aśoka had vanquished the Kaliṅga empire, we found his first edicts carved in the archaic script: "One must feed and give shelter to wanderers."

> Here, within this body, is the Ganges and Jumna…here are Prayaga and Banares—here the sun and moon. Here are the sacred places, here the pīṭhas and upa-pīṭhas. I have not seen a place of pilgrimage and an abode of bliss like my own body.

So sang Saraha, eighth century arrow-smith and tantrik Buddhist adept from Orissa on the west coast of India. His words add an unexpected twist to the pilgrim's journey, but he is not alone in his sentiments. Renowned contemplatives, fearsome yogins, and tender articulate poets have all interpreted pilgrimage in similar ways. They've mocked it as futile, belittled it, dismissed it, and reviled it for ignorance. Sixteenth century bhakti poet Mirabai, her tongue full of barbs for mechanically heedless modes of worship, declared "Banares and Ganges are found at a holy man's feet!" In Japan, Dōgen Zenji told his students, "No need to wander the dusty countries." A longstanding tradition in India discounts pilgrimage as one of the "easy" practices, contrasted to the notably tough disciplines of yoga, meditation, renunciation, or celibacy. Saraha and others of his temperament insist that Buddha himself is hidden in the practitioner's body. What use all this traveling, just to pray at a monument built over a litter of bones?

Yet, having pushed one's way through the rigors and austerities, the tough inward labors, the meditations and koans and visualizations, all those Dharma combats in the zendo or the thousands of prostrations required for Vajrayāna teachings, some people still burn with a restless curiosity that can only be satisfied by actually journeying to the legendary sites. Mirabai, it turns out, was an avid pilgrim; Saraha wandered so much no one knows quite where he practiced; and Dōgen spent twenty years marking the dusty countries with his foot soles before exhorting his students to stay home. These adepts and poets, do not forget, are using a wry topsy-turvy language meant to get under your skin. "Upside-down language," it's called in some esoteric circles. Gary Snyder has pointed out how in the literature of Zen blame is often praise in disguise. In tantra, interdiction regularly serves as the secret goad. Upside down speech, twisted utterance, hidden teachings.

And so, alert to the ironies, the Buddhist practitioner heads for north India.

Buddhism flowered in India for fifteen hundred years. It grew from a small band of wandering mendicants into a vast civilization. Princes and kings, merchants and philosophers, poets and courtesans, bandits and streetsweepers—all contributed voices and acts to a continent that was already thick with old stories. Architects, sculptors, puppeteers and painters played their roles. The splendid Mahāyāna sutras of India conjure Buddha worlds "numerous as the grains of sand on the Ganges," and today with a map you can visit thousands of unexcavated ruins. Renowned Buddhist sūtras like the *Vimalakīrti* or *Laṅkāvatara* open with a survey of those in attendance: *bhikkus* and *bhikkunīs* by the thousands, bodhisattvas by the tens of thousands, the nearly numberless gods and goddesses known to Hinduism; and *devas, nāgas, yakṣas, gandharvas, asūras, garudas, kimnaras,* and *mahoragas*—supernatural beings of every conceivable sort. Animals and ghosts appear, warlords and lepers—all are in some sense interchangable. Thus Ambapalī, former courtesan of Vaiśalī and disciple of the excellent Buddha, fashioned a song (Anne Waldman's translation):

> Once I had the body of a queen
> Now it's lowly, decrepit, an old house
> plaster falling off
> Sad but true

Partly it's this perception of splendor and squalor rubbing against one another that draws you to India: sites where Buddha "turned the wheel of Dharma" such as Vulture Peak, Magadhā, Anathapiṇḍika's garden, or Śravastī; other sites, intimately associated with Buddha's life—Lumbini, his birthplace, Bodh Gaya, where he heroically made the final push for enlightenment, Sarnath, where he gave his first instructions, and Kushanagara where he entered the great nirvana. But if you go with open eyes, there is more—charnel grounds, orphanages, sumptuous palaces and decaying forts, nuclear power plants, devastating slum sectors, holy rivers. How could you pass up an opportunity to visit the Ajanta caves, with their murals that make you weep at past splendor? The pillar-edicts set up by King Aśoka at the borders of his Buddhist kingdom? What of those splendid temples down south?

Yet a thousand years ago the Buddhist civilization that created so much grandeur disappeared. When Hsüan-tsang visited Bodh Gaya to pay homage to the legendary Bodhi tree under which Buddha had attained enlightenment, a statue of Avalokiteśvara, the bodhisattva of mercy, stood alongside it. The Chinese pilgrim recounts an old prophecy he has heard on his travels, that the earth will swallow this statue completely when Buddhism vanishes from India. With sharp unsentimental eye Hsüan-tsang then notes that the statue has already sunk to its breast in the soil of Bodh Gaya, and he gravely observes that in India Buddhism can't last longer than another 150 or 200 years.

He wasn't far off. Except for Magadhā, parts of Bengal, and distant Kashmir, between the eighth and ninth centuries Buddhism was driven from India. Twelve hundred years of Moslem then British rule have given it little room to return. The orange robe of the Buddhist pilgrim really only reappears in our own lifetime. So of that extensive, now legendary civilization, what remains in India on the eve of the twenty-first century? Shattered buildings and sculptures by the thousands, a few careful archaeological renovations, dozens of underfunded regional museums, and a million Buddhist refugees from Tibet. Yet, the legendary sites remain tender and animated. The stories associated with Buddha have lost none of their vibrancy. You have to believe that the *lokapālas*—local tutelary deities that Buddhist sculptors conscripted as protectors of the Teachings and set up as guards at the temple doors—have kept to their job.

Above all there is India herself—a teeming Buddha world. It draws pilgrims like no other nation. At the Buddhist mountain of Udhayagiri, sitting inside a hermit cave hewn from one massive boulder into the shape of a tiger's head (you go in through the jaws), I wrote in a 1993 journal:

> *I sat here once*
> *a hundred years*
> *and all the women I ever knew*
> *were like a vapor*

Even if you can't get out of Calcutta or Bombay, even if the Buddhist sites prove beyond reach, you can sit in a doorway or hermit cave, or wander on Nimtalla Ghat in Calcutta while corpses turn to ash and vapor over slow stacks of firewood. You can ponder terrible environmental destruction, or the collapse of great empires. Everything, everyone you've ever known, may seem a vapor. During Shakyamuni Buddha's own lifetime, his disciple the poet Mahākāla composed this terrible song:

This lady who cremates the dead
black as a crow—
she takes an old corpse and breaks off a thighbone,
takes an old corpse and breaks off a forearm,
cracks an old skull and sets it out
like a bowl of milk
for me to look at.

Witless brain don't you get it—?
whatever you do just
ends up here.
Get finished with karma, finished with rebirth—
no more bones of mine
on the slag heap.

It's the same meditation, twenty-five hundred years from Mahākāla to Allen Ginsberg's *Indian Journals*, their obsessive crematory description at Nimtalla Ghat that opens, "A body burning in the first ash pit."

To sit in a charnel ground and brood on impermanence—"the Way exists but not the traveler on it." To feel the skull under your face. To envision yourself the Old One, the Sick One, the Corpse. To take to the road, spurred by a Buddha's insight. To visit places others have wandered before you, them also spurred on by old stories. Maybe none of this so accomodated into life's daily round as in India these many thousand years.

Allen Ginsberg Death Notes

———

I FIRST VISITED The Naropa Institute as faculty in summer of 1989. Some-one introduced me to Allen Ginsberg as a guest invited to run a workshop on Sanskrit poetics. "What do you know about metrics of the Gāyatrī hymn?" he immediately asked, catching me off guard and without proper research book available. Gāyatrī is the name given to an old Vedic sun benediction, twenty-four syllables, which orthodox Hindus revere as a lit-eral goddess and some take as a great poetry Mother since she's the first hymn recited each day. This must have been shortly after Allen found with delight that the mighty mantra which closes *Heart Sūtra,* recited across the planet by Buddhists, has a seventeen syllable count.

Gate gate pāragate pārasaṃgate bodhi svāhā

It fascinated Allen that this all-powerful "great bright mantra" holds simple formal connection to Japanese haiku, also seventeen syllables, a terse lyric form rooted in Zen awareness of particulars. Allen was a veteran haiku practitioner and often in classes would spontaneously invent a dozen to get students warmed up. Traditional haiku exhibits the sort of irreducible clar-ity of perception Blake called for. It also presents a humble alternative to the machismo inherent in epic or the bombast of mythopoetics. Its clarity has a ringing parallel in the unparaphrasable effect of *Heart Sūtra's* closing mantra, though the latter picks up on shamanic traditions of sound-magic rather than crisp image or crystalized perception.

Allen was a keener scholar of metrics than most contemporary poets, though he buried his studies in poems, not criticism. His intuitive grip on metrical patterns was spurred by synchronicities of metric or syllable count, and in response to the *Heart Sūtra* mantra he began his series of "American Sentences," each a seventeen syllable complete poem. Bright perceptive heartbreaking funny and thoroughly American poems, they come at you from the page as if taking up squatter rights on derelict Asian traditions:

Four skinheads stand in the streetlight rain chatting under an umbrella.

Put on my tie in a taxi, short of breath, rushing to meditate.

I think Allen's interest in the Hindu Gāyatrī mantra, which millions of Brahmans chant each dawn in India, might have been an effort to find a similar metric innovation.

During July of the next six years—Naropa's summer writing program season—we'd sometimes put our heads together over the *Heart Sūtra*. Allen worked for years refining a translation he had undertaken with his companion and Buddhist teacher Gelek Rinpoche. They of course worked the Tibetan, Gelek's native tongue. But Allen wanted to know how the Sanskrit went. That was the *Sūtra*'s own native language, and Sanskrit's metrics, vocabulary, and sound values are complexly interlayered with Buddhist magical genius. Moreover, the *gate gate* mantra remains in original Sanskrit, no matter what language the Sutra's translated into—Chinese, Tibetan, Japanese, English. Those precise words and none other are "the great bright mantra that relieves suffering."

Mantra power resides (old Hindu yogic tradition) in precise articulation of all the elements of language—the syllabic rhythms, the tones and durations of sound, the points of contact between tongue, palate, teeth, and lips, the weight of the breath. Allen was both exhilirated and anxious about his translation project. Which makes sense. It was like toying with plutonium, to open the old language sorcery. This is probably why he wanted to touch in with the original Sanskrit on particular poetic coinages. He was delighted, and a bit edgy, about his line "free of all *topsy-turvy* mindsets," a good and etymologically exact rendering of the original word, *viparyāsa*. Turned about or upside down. "Imagining what is illusory or false to be real or true." Topsy-turvy gets the Buddhist psychology into lively American vernacular, and remains quite free of sanctimony. Many translations give something like "perverted views."

What was the excitement? Around Hindu and Buddhist texts of liberation? Allen must have baffled a lot of listeners when he first began to chant mantras at poetry readings to the accompaniment of Tibetan finger cymbals or Indian *shruti* box (harmonium). Professors considered him silly. News magazines made fun of him. But more than anyone else he helped us see those magic early texts as poetry, and lead us away from the peculiar Occidental weirdness which wants its religion safe in church, but sends poetry adrift and lonely to street or classroom.

Poetry and enlightenment, no difference!

If he didn't come to it on his own he would have inescapably found it in India, 1962-1963, the year he lived in Calcutta and Banaras. Everywhere you go in India you meet the Sufi tradition of *kirtan* or the Hindu *bhajan*—both of them big hootenanny sing-ins of religious music that are held on calendrical holy days or erupt spontaneously and go through the night in village squares, neighborhood temples, or at grave of some Muslim *mulla*. Dour white Protestant America needed a touch of music and ecstasy, and Allen helped bring it.

After visiting Naropa in summer of 1991 several Austrian writers from Vienna started a poetry school, the Schule für Dichtung. Allen sort of served as their guiding genius or principle advisor. I saw him insist on several occasions to the directors that they include "a meditation component" in their curriculum or he'd lose interest. There are lots of poetry programs out there, he said. Unless this one kept Buddhist mind discipline open as a poetic influence and literary point of reference, he wouldn't know how to distinguish it from dozens of other poetry schools and MFA programs around the world.

In September 1993 I went to Vienna by invitation of the Schule's directors, Ide Hintze and Christine Huber, my first trip in a dozen years to old Europa. The Schule runs its two-week autumn and spring sessions at high speed, more demanding a schedule than even the summers at Naropa, which themselves mirror Allen's youthful accomplishment-demon style. During my stay a reading was staged at Vienna's big university in a cavernous baroque Hapsburg building's lecture hall. Three of us read—Dorothea Zeeman, a spitfire Austrian prose writer in her eighties (now deceased) who supported herself writing pornography; myself accompanied by an expatriate American sitar player; and Allen.

Allen's presence sold out the hall which seats about seven hundred people. From a straight-back chair (in later years he demanded an austere seat that would keep his spine straight for readings) Allen read with bouncy animation—a dozen years younger on stage—accompanying himself on harmonium or beating time with Australian aborigine songsticks. Afterwards a group of the Schule's faculty, administrators, friends, fellow poets, went out to eat. It was late. We ended up at the Beograd, a Serbian restaurant down the same dark curved street as our hotel. History matters here—this was at the height of the ethnic cleansing war in Bosnia and there was always a nagging concern the Beograd might not be safe. Vienna lies a short automobile drive from war-torn former Yugoslavia, and tales of the mortal rivalries were coming in with travelers and refugees. On the sidewalk outside the restaurant one of our students quietly, politely excused himself, a wealthy Bosnian Muslim of impeccable manners who'd come along after the reading but would not step into a Serbian eatery. Curiously, the Beograd seems quintessentially Eastern, more Turkish than the feared and despised "Turks" of the Balkans. (Medieval stone shelters deep under Vienna still conjure war ghosts of old Islam sieges at city's edge.) Its sumptuous dining rooms struck me as gloomridden and claustrophobic, oriental carpets muting the old stone walls. Once you've gone past the front alcoves carpets blanket all windows so there's no view of the street. Brass samovars, or hammered metal wine urns sit on shelves. Decorative scimitars and shields; big dishes of meat grilled by waiters over a flame at your table on an actual sword.

Three kids from the Ukraine, about seventeen or eighteen years old, had hitchhiked nearly penniless to Vienna to hear Allen read. They looked like big handsome blond kids you'd find anywhere in the world, outfitted in leather jackets, blue jeans and boots. Quite delighted by their attentions Allen had invited them along and with characteristic generosity was buying them dinner.

Sometime into the night as we sat at a cluster of tables Allen placed his harmonium in front of him and asked the poet Bernhard Widder to turn the pages of a book while he sang. Looking the Ukranian kids in the face with immense tenderness he recited his 1971 ballad "September on Jessore Road." It's a tragic and terrible poem about refugees of the Bangladesh War, mostly poor rural Hindus, fleeing the vendettas and damnable starvation of East Pakistan for Calcutta. That Bosnian refugees were at that moment a very cruel concern in Austria added swift dimension to the song. Allen put his gospel best into it, perhaps the most moving performannce I ever heard him give. Later I questioned a few others. Yes, assuredly—few had heard him so soulful before.

I realized then how little all the fame and media attention, crowds, travel, glory meant to him when he had caught the shimmering moment of no past and no future. Three handsome teen kids from the Ukraine, saying not a word, had pulled a richer, more resounding performance out of this poetry Bodhisattva than the crowd of seven hundred cheering him earlier. Everyone's world shifted a little during the ballad. When he finished and the harmonium trailed off—that sound, half animal lament, half "lonesome whistle blow"—the group of us, maybe thirty, sat wordless. Archaic impulse, which one? the oldest—Eros—had brought Allen to that moment—the moment when love first comes upon a person and all the powers rise up. I knew then that no matter what else—the politics, the goofiness, the grouch or impatience of his later years, silly critics or fawning media—for him like for all poets Love is the original language.

You think moments like that could go on forever. But such human thoughts are inestimably foolish. Only our topsy-turvy mindsets imagine such sweetness can linger. No sooner had Allen finished than a round gray-haired man about his own age in dusty threadbare tuxedo and frayed scarlet cummerbund—the house musician, a gypsy—came hustling over, a battered violin in his hands. Eyes bright with challenge, he called energetically to Allen in loud German, grabbing attention of all the eaters and drinkers. Now it was his turn, he let us know. Allen had lit the place up with music. It was this man's turf, he was house musician, and he would respond with his own piece.

Theatrically, everyone watching him, he released the bright high string from his violin. Stretching it out perpendicular with his left hand, he fixed the instrument under his chin, then began lifting dozens of weird sounds, hundreds of them, alone and in sequence, as he bobbed and bent and stretched and tormented that one string with his bow. Someone told me it is a longstanding East European practice, the evocation of bird sounds—calls, squawks, chirps, croaks, caws. He was terrific. Everyone cheered and he bowed with the largesse of a man at home.

That night I had a dream which I jotted down. A week or two later I wrote it up.

Vienna Dream

I meet the poet Allen Ginsberg at a Vienna cafe. He has hidden himself off at a side table behind a potted palm. Huge Egyptian fronds bend over and his black harmonium sits on the table. "No difference between poetry and meditation," he is saying distractedly as I squeeze onto a bench alongside. "They work the same way. Poetry and mediation." His eyes are painfully sad. I don't think he wanted to reach this conclusion. He looks so small and orderly in shirtsleeves and conservative tie, almost a college professor. I should be polite but I'm too young, he knows it, his eyes get sadder. I'm too young for what he's trying to say—

"But you meditate to end suffering," I protest, "calm your heart, keep the guru's command." Allen sighs, he knows what's next. "While poetry—" I'm too strident, something's wrong, "you write poetry to get famous, travel, have fun, sleep with boys, be glamorous...." It's terribly difficult, his shoulders are slumped. I've gone too far. There's something I don't get. He stares at the marble tabletop under the palm fringes, very gloomy, like Freud, he knows too much, we're in Vienna, some political disaster's about to occur. "Poetry and meditation. No difference." He hunches over his coffee. I realize he's trying to warn me about something....

The old coyote. A cranky Bodhisattva up to familiar tricks. His sly history-burdened gloom to counter my dreamself's over-earnest dualism. Pushing the inseparability of poetry and wisdom. Not so different from earlier days when he'd inquired about metrics of the Gāyatrī hymn so he could possibly accomplish a modern poetry retrieval from ancient Sanskrit verse-patterns. Now he'd come and slipped past gates of the dream to make an old point.

In Buddhism the teachers often show up in what's called the *saṃbhogakāya*, an apparition body, described in old texts as mutable, shapeshifting, dreamlike. Check out the biography of Milarepa, or abundant tantric tales of teachers and students who whisk around in dreams and mysterious trances. Consider the Sūtra recited by lay buddha Vimalakīrti, who lives in a "ten-foot room" but seats uncounted thousands of sentient creatures inside, without any discomfort or jostling, to hear a few choice words of poetry wisdom. These people now are Allen's proper companions I suppose.

We'll miss him. Summers at Naropa, no big classes singing Blake or Shelley in white tent on dry lawn under sycamores. No burgundy colored Mont Blanc pen looping careful thoughts at Rocky Mountain seminar table for student instruction. No Allen off evenings at summer residence Varsity Townhouse boiling up macrobiotic meals—cauldrons of rice & buckwheat, organic carrots, kale or summer squash with miso. Always obligatory to eat a bowl when you stop by for talk. He made vast unrefusable quantities be-cause—because he wanted to feed everyone! Then he'd quietly, impeccably clean up after you left.

One summer an assistant went out to buy cookware for his kitchen. She returned with a Teflon frying pan. Allen glanced at it and growled, "You think poets don't know how to do their own dishes?"

Whether it was keeping the CIA honest on drugs, protesting Rocky Flats plutonium production site or USA war mongering, assisting fellow poets and friends with money and generous words, or giving the dope on cigarettes—Allen's job as poet activist and Buddhist practitioner seems to have been exactly that: to feed everyone, and then to do the dishes.

These thoughts blown after you, Allen, into the shimmering void.

9 April 1997
Sukhāvatī Ceremony
Dorje Dzong
Boulder, Colorado

Ramprasad Sen's Poems to the Goddess

This essay served as the preface to the second edition of Grace and Mercy in Her Wild Hair: Selected Poems to the Mother Goddess by Ramprasad Sen, *translated by Leonard Nathan and Clinton Seely (Hohm Press: Prescott, 1999).*

AT THE MOLTEN magnetic core of our planet, or in some tellings of it, at the base of our own spines, is a terrible burning ground of Life and Death. There, on the reclining corpse of her husband, the Mother of all things—Gaia or Tellus, Kālī or Durgā—performs a primal unclad dance, slow and insistent as geomorphic force. While She exults in Her own sport, nearby flames devour the tender creatures to whom She has given birth. Vultures and feral dogs pick at the leftover corpses. It is a frightful ground to those who glimpse it, but it is the field on which the Śaktas, devotees of the Goddess, gather to worship.

Do not imagine the Śaktas to be some alienated turn-of-the millennium cult addicted to video-game imagery. It is likely they are the inheritors of insights that reach deep into the Paleolithic. What they study is the complicated mix of violent and benign forces that govern our planet. In Bengal, where the Śaktas are most numerous, they and their beliefs are called *guhya*: covered, concealed, sequestered, mysterious; underground; the hidden recess. For centuries this term has been applied to caves and grottos as well as to the female sexual organ. No wonder the Śaktas of Bengal stay underground. They have glimpsed a terrible secret. It is that the Great Mother of all beings in one of her truest moods is a shameless, naked, wilderness goddess, companioned by jackals, stoned out of her senses on blood or ganja, who performs a slow orgiastic dance while her children die.

In recent years Western cultures have learnt a great deal about their own matrilocal origins. The way has been led by feminist scholars, who have done heroic work stripping off centuries of wrong-headed social beliefs. Likewise, studies by Marija Gimbutas and others have publicized the hundreds of stone-age female fertility statuettes found across Europe and the Near East. These figurines, with their ample hips, buttocks and breasts, have begun to present a human self-image that seems both postmodern and utterly archaic. The Willendorf Venus, on display in the state museum in Vienna, has become a celebrated icon of a postmodern Europe. There are also the renowned Shila-na-gig (cunt shrines) of Ireland, as well as female sex-organ images on cave walls in the Dordogne. "The Goddess is Awake and Magic is Afoot," pertly declares a Wiccan bumper sticker.

It is unlikely however that the Goddess, the Great Mother, is to be known by the study of comparative religion (though this may tell us many interesting things), by searching out archaic amulets, or by posting a bumper sticker.

> Who knows
> What She truly is?
>
> Ramprasad says: If She decides
> To be kind, this misery will pass.

Ramprasad Sen (ca. 1720-1780), who lived out his days in a small village north of Calcutta, may be Her finest surviving poet. I say surviving because there is no way to retrieve the many songs to the Goddess that vanished before humans learnt to put speech into writing. Nor can anyone restore the manuscripts lost from monsoon India when fungus, insects, water or fire devoured them. Or those destroyed by intolerant clerics in Europe, North Africa, or Mesoamerica. Of what remains, there is much we are lucky to have at all. For this reason I cannot tell you with what gratitude I welcome back into print these fine translations by Leonard Nathan and Clinton Seely. Their task has been a difficult one—to move between languages as different as 18th century Bengali and contemporary American English, to catch in our own tongue some of the chewable slangy quality of songs preserved "on the street" for 200 years. And most difficult of all, to convey Ramprasad Sen's tough, wry, wheedling, brave, and utterly vulnerable manner of speech.

Rereading these poems, published in 1982 but out of print for over a decade, I have been moved again by their razor sharp honesty. They have brought in their wake a cascade of images, a specific iconography, that sweeps me back to the enormous, thronged, madcap Kālī temple in Calcutta that gave the modern city its name. It hardly matters that Ramprasad considered priestly ritual, worship of statues, animal slaughter, recitation of prayers, or the lighting of lamps, to be largely devoid of merit. The temple at Kalikatha is something! It could be an architecture built from his poems.

Should you ever get to Calcutta, go search out the temple some evening, in the south part of the city away from the noise and industrial soot of downtown. With its surrounding maze of boisterous colorful shops, trinket stalls, kitchens, brassy shrines, fortune tellers, beggars, lepers, energetic hucksters, and priests, the Kālī temple is a great microcosm of life and a steady destination for pilgrims. Here the earth, where a severed finger of the Great Mother once fell, is chewed by thousands of feet, hoofs, and automobile tires. It is a vast cauldron of mud and spittle, cook oil and motor oil, dust, food, shit, bright scarlet flower petals and spattered blood that's a bit darker. Lines of busses and taxis idle their motors by the front entrance. Yet it makes a compelling refuge from present-day Calcutta. Somehow the crowds and confusion make sense when you draw near the Goddess.

The temple has a viewing platform where you go, if you haven't fasted and purified yourself the requisite number of days to take *darshan* (spiritual viewing) with the precious long-tongued Kālī image. In 1993 an official sign hung above:

> It is Forbidden
> to deceive Pilgrims
> while Ceremonies
> are in Progress

Facing that sign is like facing Ramprasad's poetry. It forces the mind towards a paradox you can't ever escape. Don't think you can get through this world without losing everything! Don't imagine the Goddess plays by your rules! The single most compelling quality of Ramprasad Sen is how he recklessly confronts the endless round of deceptions—deceptions by others, of oneself by oneself, of even the most earnest seeker by the Mother who spins out her web of Māyā.

Orthodox Hindus have generally looked on Goddess cults with a mixture of condescension and distaste. In anthropological terms you could say it's the dominant culture's anxiety around native people who still follow old telluric ways. More directly, it's got to do with the mutability and chaos of the feminine itself, which anyone finds if not scary at least pretty baffling. Here's a ninth century Sanskrit poem by the amiable Bengali poet, Yogeśvara. It's a sort of ethnographic snapshot of India's indigenous culture (my translation).

> The tribesmen dispatch
> creature after
> living creature to Durgā,
> Goddess who dwells in a craggy wilderness grotto.
> They slosh the blood on a field-spirit tree.
> Then joined by their women at dusk
> go wild to the gourd-lute
> stopping just to pass liquor around—
> the old way—
> in a *bilva* fruit husk.

This kind of Earth Goddess orgy, no doubt familiar to Ramprasad, still takes place. I have seen in the hills of Bihar and Orissa the little shrines in the groves, with their well-trampled dance ground, the sacrifice-posts, the spirit trees wrapped in bright playful fabric. Clay pots hang in the palm trees to catch sap for the liquor. But please do not rush off to see these things! It was the genius of Ramprasad's poetry to lift the old tribal practices and in a cosmopolitan and psychologically astute manner intertwine them with the tantrika's belief that we animate an inner spiritual landscape. The secret of his poetry is that worship of the Goddess is a powerful personal drama—a devotional yoga—in which the creatures sacrificed are one's own fondest delusions. In which the celebratory dance-ground is one's own liberated mind.

The evidence suggests that Ramprasad sung his poems and never made books. The people who first wrote them down treated the manuscripts as spiritually potent objects. In 1853 a Bengali poet, Iśvaracandra Gupta, described his decades-long search for copies of Ramprasad poems.

> Works of his which had been collected together earlier have by now almost disappeared, because in those days people used to guard them carefully like some secret mantra, not showing them to anyone even at the cost of their lives, bringing them out only at puja time to decorate with flowers and sandalwood paste, as some people still do today, and though we would have given all we had we were not able to obtain any of the verses. Hidden in this way they have become completely destroyed. Worms and other insects ate them, moisture decomposed them, fire burned them, they were used by the impotent as charms to secure beautiful women or long life....
>
> (translated by Malcolm McLean)

For good or for ill, things that for centuries were hidden away, or remained the possession of a particular people, are now out where anyone with a little effort and the price of a book can find them. This is true of Ramprasad's tantric poetry, which you could say was hidden on the streets of Bengal in the mouths of largely non-literate singers for so many decades. Now those poems come out and speak with refreshing honesty to the human condition. Readers of English are privileged to see them.

I believe there are reasons certain teachings do not get handed out indiscriminately. Why some old poetries are jealously guarded. Perhaps it is unwise to talk in too loud a voice of Kālī's odd habits—the fierce drunkenness, the charnel ground howling, the unlicensed barebreasted dance on a corpse. Maybe such talk should wait till the children have gone off to bed. That's the time to pull Ramprasad Sen's poetry off the shelf and see what it holds. The teachings are difficult, but they might set you free.

Manuscript Fragments & Eco-Guardians
The Estate of Sanskrit Poetry

Nature Literacy

WITHIN SANSKRIT POETRY and the related vernacular lyrics that comprise
North India's classical tradition, a quality I find more and more compelling
is the deep, studied regard shown the natural world. In our turn-of-the
millennia period an intense debate is in progress over the status of wilderness areas and the importance of non-human species. The urgency of concerns about wildlands and the disappearance of species across the planet—
along with a stubborn archaic belief that one of the poet's jobs is to articulate the unique presence of birds and mammals, insects or river systems—
has put contemporary poets on the alert for insights into nature or wilderness that distant artistic traditions might offer. I am convinced the best
Sanskrit poems contain the tracks of something instructive. Rooted in Paleolithic habits of observation, they balance a fine-tuned eco-literacy with
a cosmopolitan delight in language, social patterns, and erotic behavior.
Wild creatures were daily familiars to the Sanskrit poets, who studied
them with a close unsentimental eye, observed how closely implicated
they were in human behavior, and noted how parallel passions and enthusi-
asms animated them.

A poem attributed to Apanāgara, found in King Hāla's second-century
anthology *Gāhākosa*, written in a vernacular of Maharashtra State:

> Stag and doe
> hard short lives
> ranging the forest for
> water and grass

they don't
betray each other they're
loyal
till death

For a North American poet working to become nature-literate on
home territory it is of enormous interest to see with what ease creatures
of the natural world can become citizens of standing in the poem. The Sanskrit vocabulary for flowers and trees in particular is abundant and botani-
cally accurate. Happening on this tradition at the remove of a thousand
years, one might at first glance miss the precision of detail, but non-human
elements of the landscape were carefully regulated inside the Sanskrit lyric.
Poets worked specific flowers or blooming trees, particular birds, animals,
or phases of weather, into compressed cultural cyphers. I don't mean they
were employed symbolically. Rather, they provided a customary setting for
the poem, instantly recognizable to a reasonably well traveled resident of
India. Mere hint of fragrance off a nearby forested hill told not only in
what calendar moment of what season the poem was located, but its
bioregional particulars as well. A single detail could evoke a constellation
of human relationships (also calibrated to the season), a precise mood, and
of course vivid moments echoed from earlier poems.

There's good evidence this use of native creatures came into classical
Sanskrit from the somewhat earlier Tamil tradition to the south. Classical
Tamil poets (ca. 100 BCE-250 CE), writing in a Dravidian tongue, devised
for their intricately erotic short poems an alphabet of natural elements
which they calibrated to distinct landscapes—what we now call bioregions.
By invoking the name of a single plant or animal native to a known habitat,
they would summon an image at once natural, cultural, regionally precise,
and resonant with a particular emotion. The Tamil poets identified five wilderness regions; current natural history would classify them as montane,
riparian meadow, forest, littoral shoreline, and arid scrubland. Each landscape set the scene for a particular erotic mood. Plant companions are so
abundantly featured that A.K. Ramanujan's good book of translations, *Poems of Love and War*, includes a botanical index which reads like the "List of

Plants" which stands as an appendix to Henry David Thoreau's *The Maine Woods.*

In a looser way the Sanskrit poets, from the founding of the Gupta Empire in the year 320, used this type of alphabet for their own lyric, introducing the kind of attention to seasonal changes in various bioregions that has been the stuff of natural history, and superimposing on the natural orders a sophisticated psychology of human life. Regional plants, weather patterns, bird migration, animal instincts, seasonal cycles: all were used emblematically. Though the intention was to provoke distinct emotional tones, their use lends sound testimony to Ezra Pound's counsel: "the natural object is always the adequate symbol."

Aside from a hundred rather fierce lyrics by Bhartṛhari (circa seventh century)—who was very likely a celebrated linguist and a bark-clad yogin at different times in his life—little Sanskrit poetry was written by hermits. The poets formed a professional guild—some doing double-time as philosophers or scholars—and rarely chose to live outside human settlements or to develop yogic powers among the wild, non-human orders. The fact that poems minutely familiar with nature were not written by recluses gives Sanskrit short poems a different flavor from those of the adjacent Chinese tradition: the settings or landscapes seem closer to home; there are few brooding mountain escarpments, few unvisited gorges along thundering rivers.

In Sanskrit lyric the human and non-human orders seem linked in unsensational daily intimacy. Local villages flocked with birds in flowering trees. The whiff of odors from a nearby forest grove. Farmland crops or native grasses in fertile alluvial soil. Sweet smelling blossoms along a village path. To put it another way: what flowering creeper shares the details of your life because you walk past it every day to fetch water? What pliant reed did you collect one moonlit spring night in order to weave a couch for your lover?

Transcendentalist Tracks

The tricky, many-forked paths a poet takes into other centuries and other literatures are hard to trace. Sanskrit poetry—indeed the thorny old language itself—seems a curious place to end up, and it's hard to be sure how I got there. There's a good poem by Dharmakīrti—it has a postmodern taste—that might serve as an entry point. Dharmakīrti was a Buddhist scholar from South India who late in the seventh century wrote seven razor-witted treatises on Buddhist logic, several sūtra commentaries, and an unknown number of lyric poems, of which a handful survive. One of them reads:

> No one visible up ahead,
> no one approaches
> from behind.
> Not a footprint on the road.
> Am I alone?
> This much is clear—
> the path the ancient
> poets opened
> is choked with brush,
> and I've long since left
> the public thoroughfare.

I grew up in Transcendentalist country: the pre-revolutionary townships that spread west of Boston. This meant that as a child I became familiar in a native way with the forests and meadows Henry David Thoreau surveyed. I dodged watchful rangers to swim the ponds he washed in or wrote about, and I lived on close terms with the little holy places of Emerson, Margaret Fuller, the Alcott girls and their eccentric philosophic father.

An airy mixture of Asiatic books and thoughtful Romantic philosophies (which read like poetry) hung over the region. Thanks to early curators Ananda Coomaraswamy and Ernest Fenollosa, local museums offered world-class collections of Indian sculpture and Chinese landscape paintings. These exposed viewers to archetypes of consciousness hewn in Indian sandstone, or forested crags rendered in Chinese ink. To stand in the presence of these was to catch a cool glimpse of the way one's own mind was fashioned.

Thoreau had been exposed to something similar, though in a rougher more solitary way. In *Walden* he tells of waking at dawn and walking to the pond's edge to collect water. When he gets to the shore, time and space collapse for a moment and he catches sight of a Hindu arriving just that moment at the bank of the Ganges, filling his own little water pot. This leap—what could it mean? That *Bhagavad-gītā*, the *Upaniṣads*, some Buddhist sūtras, the Hindu *Purānas* were, by the middle of the nineteenth century, cross-fertilizing among New England hemlock, maple and oak? That even the geographic error solidified in use of the word "Indian" for this continent's native peoples expresses some unarticulated karmic link between North American landscapes and South Asian texts? Emerson and old man Alcott thought so.

It was the holy books of Sanskrit I encountered first. Full of thunder and wind, craggy metaphysics, humorous folklore, shivery insight, they felt like poetry. No matter the available translations were largely in a not very lively prose. When I settled down to get what I could of Sanskrit into my head, it was because the familiar translations, many from last century, no longer felt close enough. What had those British and German philologists left out? Looking into their translations I glimpsed something tawny, a muscular flex back of the language: like snapping your glance around in the forest—an instant too late to identify the creature that's gone into the trees. At the time I did not know there was also a classical tradition of poetry—secular, tenderly amorous, refined and instructively nature literate—lying in wait. As an American this would have been hard to know.

There have been few good translations of Sanskrit lyric poetry. Mostly there's been indifference, occasionally disdain, shown towards Sanskrit verse. Because there are no good translations? Or is it the other way around, that a colonialist *hauteur* has produced third-rate translation? Introducing his Chinese anthology of 1929, *The Jade Mountain: The 300 Poems of the T'ang Dynasty,* Witter Bynner states, "I doubt I could ever feel any affection for the ornate, entranced poetry of India." This was seventeen years after the first Imagist manifestos: two decades of Ezra Pound, H.D., Williams, Marianne Moore and a handful of other writers working out that lean American hunger for poems shorn of adornment. Few adjectives could have been more damning than *ornate* and *entranced*.

The English translations Bynner would have seen by 1929 could only have backed up his estimate. They're mostly worthless. British or American scholars put Sanskrit poems—surprisingly compressed, fleet-footed and alert in the originals—into Tennysonian iambics. Furthermore, for complex reasons most translators seemed to require three or four times as many English words as Sanskrit. Given the distance between the two languages—one heavily inflected, the other quite analytic—I realize it would be nearly impossible to define what constitutes a "word." Nonetheless a survey of bilingual books on my shelf reveals that translations of Chinese poetry use only one and a half to two English words for each Chinese ideogram—though the originals show no verb tenses or pronouns and not much in the way of prepositions, all of which translators into English supply. Why such wordiness in Sanskrit translations?

A long-winded translation of a sprightly poem—Chinese, Indian, or any other—misses the one thing that counts: the poetry. John Dryden said it for all of us: "I cannot, without some indignation, look on an ill copy of an excellent original ...a good poet is no more like himself in a dull translation, than his carcass would be to a living body." When in my studies I encountered *kāvya* (Sanskrit's short lyric poetry), I was unprepared to like it and so was surprised to see how much vigor it had. Only two modern scholars have recognized this vigor, gone to the poetry on its own turf, and done good work: Daniel H.H. Ingalls, who has devoted himself to it and written the best overview of Sanskrit poetry; and Barbara Stoller Miller, who throughout her life produced clean, modern translations based on impeccable scholarship. Without their efforts, the trail might still be lost.

It is instructive to consider the effect China and Japan have had on American poetry. By contrast, India seems nearly invisible. There are two, possibly three Sanskrit words in Pound's *Cantos*. *The Wasteland* has three, all drawn from a single episode in the *Upaniṣads* (Eliot, interested in Buddhism, studied Sanskrit as an undergraduate at Harvard). Only with Kenneth Rexroth's post-WWII poetry does Indian mythopoetics enter Anglo-American poetry in a compelling way.

Few Sanskrit scholars appear to like the poetry. The standard reference books—British scholars compiled them during colonial times—treat it with dismay or outright contempt. Closer to our own day, D.D. Kosambi, an influential literary Marxist and co-editor of the important 12th century anthology *Subhāṣita-ratna-koṣa,* dismisses it for other reasons. Following Plekhanov's theory of literary production, Kosambi maintains that good poetry can only be written by newly emergent classes that are advancing the means of production. The Sanskrit poets were courtiers or courtesans, scholars or school teachers—not labor revolutionaries. Their poetry, according to Kosambi's analysis, "necessarily carries with the rank beauty of an orchid the corresponding atmosphere of luxury, parasitism, decay."

If the professionals don't like it, readers will be indifferent. Predictably, the original texts remain hard to find. Only a half-dozen libraries in our country have a workable collection. Where I live, along the front range of Colorado's Rocky Mountains, we're a thousand miles—the width of India—from the nearest Sanskrit collection of note. Luckily a few dealers in Calcutta and Delhi have helped turn up useful books; but many volumes are hopelessly scarce: they went out of print in Bombay or Poona a hundred years ago.

Ragged Manuscripts

Classical Sanskrit poetry was written over the course of about eight hundred years, beginning approximately 320 CE with the founding of the Gupta Empire. During those centuries, Indian civilization reached its height. The culture was abundant and cosmopolitan, drawing Chinese pilgrims, Arab merchants, and Greek philosophers to its courts. Most of India's exquisite classical sculpture, architecture, and mural painting, the manuals of science, erotics, theater, linguistics, and philosophy, were also produced during this period. All these arts came to a violent end during the eleventh and twelfth centuries, when Muslim warriors of solid military capability rode on horseback through the Kyber Pass and down onto the Gangetic Plains, taking control of the cities and highways. They drove out the Buddhists who had compiled extensive libraries in their *vihāras* (universities). Some manuscripts managed to survive, hidden away, especially in the South. But throughout the North the *vihāras* were sacked or burnt, and the libraries vanished.

Buddhist monks lucky enough to escape fled to Tibet, carrying what manuscripts they could: sūtra literature and Buddhist exegesis, accounts of Buddhist kings and yogins, but also volumes of secular writings. One of the notable examples is the *Subhāṣita-ratna-koṣa,* compiled between 1100 and 1130 by a likable scholar, Vidyākara, who served as abbot of Jagaddala *vihāra* in Bengal. A Buddhist monk with a keen ear for poetry, he saw no contradiction between his religious training and the teeming, playful, erotic poems he collected. His anthology—translated in full by Daniel Ingalls as *An Anthology of Sanskrit Court Poetry*—is open-minded and tolerant. Its 1,738 poems include hundreds of erotic epigrams, cameos of tender moments, portraits of lovers, children, poor people, rich people, animals, and accounts of the seasons. There's wit, despair, humor, irony, bitterness, affection; many of the poems are love poems, as good as those written in any language.

Vidyākara's anthology was entirely lost until this century, when two explorers a few years apart happened upon a readable twelfth-century palm-leaf manuscript, probably Vidyākara's personal copy, at the Ngor monastery in Tibet, about a day's journey by foot from Shigatse. First, in 1934, Rahula Sankrityayana—an Indian pandit, a good scholar and a good Sanskritist, possibly up in Tibet as a British spy—found the manuscript in a barn attached to the monastery. A few years later Giuseppe Tucci, the noted Italian art collector and scholar of Buddhism, also came across it. Each managed to produce under challenging conditions photographic plates of very poor quality ("execrable," says one account), and to transport them out of Tibet.

Working from these plates, which they compared against photos, manuscript fragments, and more recent anthologies housed in libraries in Nepal and India that held some of the same poems, D.D. Kosambi and fellow Indian scholar V. V. Gokhale managed to edit a clean edition for Harvard University Press's Oriental Series. Here, from Kosambi's 1957 introduction to the poems, is a representative estimate on the estate of the old poems:

> A chance still remains of getting better materials from Tibet, including the original manuscript or good new photographs.... This was in fact promised me at Peking in 1952 by the authorities of the People's Republic of China.... (However) Tibet being completely au-

tonomous in such purely internal matters, the new evidence will not be forthcoming as long as the manuscripts remain sacred possessions of the monasteries, to be worshiped unread, or sold in fragments for pilgrims to use as charms. There is no doubt that the Tibetans themselves will soon develop a modern scientific attitude towards their priceless treasures, which are India's treasures too. This implies the development of systematic archaeology, which will open up images and stupas in which many manuscripts may have been immured.   (p. xxi)

Two things strike me in this little account. First, though many went unread, the old Sanskrit manuscripts were considered sacred items. That Tibetans regarded them as holy is both why they were preserved and why outsiders rarely got wind of them. The other notable thing is that decades before global tourism entered the Himalayas—trekkers in Gore-Tex, college students with granola bars, high-tech trophy mountaineers, international dealers in cheaply bought antiquities, and all sorts of other travelers willing to trade hard cash for old goods in the little mountain villages—manuscripts were already being broken apart by monks and sold off to visitors, or more interestingly, being ritually inserted into religious icons. Might entire pages of high quality Sanskrit poetry, tied into bricklike amulets, be lying unread inside bronze icons or little prayer boxes?

I have instant sympathy with Buddhist mountain pilgrims, polyandrous Tibetan mothers, Tantric yogins, and energetic yak-herding yoginīs who worship texts without needing to read them. They have preserved oral teachings that may prove more valuable than written texts. They've maintained techniques of personal insight, religious magic, and social ceremony our planet dearly needs. They've saved fragile manuscripts. Still, I like to imagine that one day in the twenty-first century a sheaf of unknown poems by Lady Śīlābhaṭṭārikā, grown ragged over the centuries, will be recovered from the base of a bare-breasted bronze Tārā and ably translated.

We know the sad history though. Two years after Professor Kosambi wrote his account, Chinese soldiers moved artillery into Lhasa, the Dalai Lama fled, and the People's Army set out on a savage wrecking spree which may not yet be over. Statues were destroyed or melted down for

bullion; others were hustled away at great personal risk by Tibetans and secured in remote caves. Tibet's "modern archaeology" seems no closer than
it did in 1957. When it does come, if it does, archaeologists and scientists
will need to work alongside knowledgable lamas who can preside over any
excavations, recording of lost texts, and subsequent re-sealing of holy images and stūpas.

Lady Śīlābhaṭṭārikā's Poem

Six short poems, distributed through several anthologies, bear the
name of Śīlābhaṭṭārikā, who most likely lived in the ninth century. Whatever else she wrote has been lost. Her best-known one is of a quick, almost
unendurable beauty. If one believes Śīlā to have written it from direct personal experience, she would have lived as a young woman in one of the villages or towns along the Narmada River, close to the Vindhya mountain
range in West India. Her poem occurs in at least two versions; this is the
one from a fourteenth-century anthology, the *Paddhati* of Śārngadhara:

> Nights of jasmine & thunder,
> torn petals,
> wind in the tangled *kadamba* trees—
> nothing has changed.
> Spring comes again and we've
> simply grown older.
> In the cane groves of Narmada River
> he deflowered my
> girlhood before we were
> married.
> And I grieve for those faraway nights
> we played at love
> by the water.

According to ancient and modern critics, this version has a flaw. Poetic
convention does not permit the *mālatī*, a jasmine, to bloom in *Caitra*, the lunar month of March-April, or spring. If Śīlābhaṭṭārikā got the botany wrong,
the critics' complaints would be a sound eco-critique of her best poem.

Did Śīlābhaṭṭārikā herself make this mistake? Or could her poem, going into the *Paddhati* five hundred years after she wrote it, have been rewritten by someone unfamiliar with poetic convention or botanical detail? Śīlā certainly recalls the *malati* blooming—blooming that season she made love all night on the riverbank as a girl. But having aged, has she confused the lunar month of Caitra with another? Mislocated the event?

Sanskrit's enormous vocabulary is full of words with complex overtones or several related but distinct meanings woven into each other. Because the meanings are sometimes linked by something as subtle as a fragrance, no word by word translation can hope to catch the *rasa*, the mood or flavor of a good verse. I find several early lexicographers give *mālatī* the additional meaning of "virgin." The scent of jasmine, the newly opened flower releasing its fragrance. Without denying the botanical fact, the image could stand for the poet herself on those faraway nights of Caitra.

The other version is from Vidyākara's anthology:

> The one who deflowered me
> is still my lover
> the moondrenched nights haven't changed.
> Scent from the newly
> bloomed *mālatī*
> blows in from the Vindhya hills
> and the girl is still me.
> But her heart?
> It grieves for those nights
> we stole off and made love forever
> in the riverside cane.

Having gone deep into the jasmine-scented darkness, deep into the dictionary, deep into the poet's rhythm (set in a meter provocatively called *śārdūla-vikrīḍitā*, "tiger's play"), both poems grip me. Which would you give up: the moondrenched nights (*candra-garba-niśa*) or the breeze scented with torn kadamba blossoms (*kadamba-anilaḥ*)? If you could have only one which would it be: the Vindhya Mountains or the Narmada River?

The Sanskrit short poem is a compressed moment of bedrock human emotion set into a briefly and accurately sketched landscape. Śīlā's temperament and training would have required a strict economy of language to reach that conjunction. Perhaps to write both mountains and river into a single poem was not in the Sanskrit grain. But the wild fragrant nights, wind off the hills, flowering branches and moonlight; the abandon with which a girl takes her first lover; the bittersweet recollections of a middle-aged woman looking back on it all—it seems hardly extravagant to make two separate poems. What does it matter the critics consider one a bit ragged?

Nature Sentinels

From the *Kavikaṇṭhābharaṇam*, a twelfth-century verse treatise on poetic training by Kśemendra, comes this good counsel:

> With his own
> eyes a poet
> observes the shape of a leaf.
> He knows how to make
> people laugh
> and studies the nature of each living thing.
> The features of ocean and mountain,
> the motion of sun, moon and stars.
> His thoughts turn with the seasons.
> He goes among
> different peoples
> learning their landscapes,
> learning their languages.

There's no explicit scholarship to cite, but it is my own belief that the way the Sanskrit poets continually and accurately named their trees, creepers, rivers, mountain ranges, and weather patterns reveals an archaic, "preliterate" habit of language. Recurring in endless variants, phrases like "newly opened jasmine," "black clouds mount the horizon," or "wind from the Vindhya mountains" did not originate as descriptions of nature, but were active spells set loose to summon the particular spirit controlling the event. The poetic handbooks of India, which were carefully consulted—their exacting rules cover not only grammar and metrics but also natural history—have similar roots in the customs of people who hunt and garden. They keep watch over the local calendar: animal migration and fertility, plant growth, weather cycles, river floodings.

The composers of the Vedic hymns (ca. 1700 BCE) bequeathed to India a treasury of ritual verse that summons the forces of a dramatic wilderness: thunder, wind, boiling clouds, sky-rending bolts of lightning, a mysterious female forest spirit, even frogs. We know that those early *Ṛsis* or poet-priests were specialists who compelled local spirits by ritual use of plants, animal products, and fire. After a lapse of two thousand years, the poets of classical Sanskrit took up the old energies and redirected them, bringing the poem to focus on specifically human affairs and old erotic imperatives. The archaic grain was not lost: the innovation was simply to lay patterns of human life across the earlier mythic orders.

From this perspective, most collections of classical Sanskrit poetry can be seen as ritual accounts of the Indian year. The short poems come down to us in anthologies ranging from collections of a hundred lyrics to over four thousand. A quick glance shows how often the anthologists ordered their books into seasonal and diurnal cycles, and patterned both alongside or on top of the rounds of human life: erotic, social, or simply biological. You can therefore read the anthologies as almanacs. The habits of animals, the tree groves, the seasonally flooding rivers, clouds bulking over the mountains, the fragrant blossoms—as in so much old poetry these are the good companions, spirit guides on the human journey.

And the task of the poem? One of the oldest. To bring humans into right relation with denizens of the plant, animal, or geological kingdoms. Some of these creatures took up lodging in the Sanskrit poem, others went into sculpture, architecture, painting, folklore, and the varied range of Hindu and Buddhist texts. A popular term applied to them was *lokapāla*, "place guardian," protective figures that formally watch over the eight directions or the neighborhood holy places: a temple door, a clear little runnel dropping out of the forest, a hillside grotto, the meadow at a bend in the river. Local and cosmological, they are "world guardians," sentinels of place.

What the Sanskrit poets accomplished was to secularize these sentinels and then to regard them with the naturalist's careful eye. It gives their writings a precise sense of ecology that seems nearly contemporary. Perhaps Kśemendra, Śīlābhaṭṭārikā, and their comrades—their writings scattered through fragmentary old manuscripts—can offer a few useful models as North Americans develop a poetry both cosmopolitan and minutely adapted to our own terrain. A poetry of romance, stout friendship, the sharp unforgettable image, the easy native wit. But also bristling with residents of our own ecosystems: cacti and piñon trees, granite outcroppings, migratory songbirds, the hardy native flowers of our upland meadows.

Won't the poets of old India clap their hands when they hear of it.

Bardo of Lost Mammals

The editors at Tricycle: The Buddhist Journal *commissioned this piece for an Autumn 2001 issue. They were compiling a feature section in which various writers and Buddhist teachers discussed the notion of* bardo. *The term bardo is Tibetan. It first came to the attention of Western students of Buddhist thought with W.Y. Evans-Wentz's 1937 translation of* Bardo Thödol—*in his version* The Tibetan Book of the Dead. *Bardo is the condition in which consciousness finds itself between lifetimes: an after death or before birth state. Similar concepts occur throughout the literatures of South and East Asia, and in fact around the planet. In the 1970s a popular handbook for experimentation with acid and mescaline by Timothy Leary and others,* The Psychedelic Experience, *took Evans-Wentz's book for its model. At this point the term bardo has entered American vernacular. The spell-check function on my Macintosh accepts it.*

> What but the wolf's tooth whittled so fine
> the fleet limbs of the antelope?
> —ROBINSON JEFFERS

SOME BUDDHISTS maintain that every moment is a bardo state & every living or sentient creature is being incessantly reborn. I think it not a stretch to hold this tenet in one hand, in the other the Bodhisattva vow as it appears in *Diamond Sūtra*. That singular vow, one of literatures most sinewy passages, and which articulates the resolve at the core of Buddhist practice, makes explicit that all creatures of whatever description, seen or unseen, named or unnamed, are to be brought with us on the Great Journey. This means mammals, birds, fish, plants, bacteria—whatever form a sentient creature appears in.

But other evidence has been coming in at an alarming rate: sentient beings of every possible description are getting snuffed out across the planet. In fact the pace of species extinction is proceeding much faster than in any previous period of loss (such as when the dinosaurs went down). What's painful is that this current catastrophe is entirely due to human behavior. Most of the critters vanishing under the impact of out-of-control human civilizations have not even been catalogued by biologists. A friend puts it poignantly: "They have no names."

Wild lands are being cut, ploughed, bulldozed, and paved as I type and you read this little bardo piece. Ten years ago the Amazon rainforests were going "every forty seconds / the size of a football field / off to the lumber boats," a piece of data so disheartening and vivid that after a decade the phrase still pulses in one's mind. Yet in response there has been an encouraging & sometimes effective counter movement, not just to protect vanishing species & threatened watersheds, but in many regions across the planet to reintroduce them. That's why I sometimes tell friends, "Wilderness is not in the past but the future." What could this mean? Could the phrase be a koan—one unexplainable even to myself? My guess is it has something to do with humans as a species having a much clearer, better informed, more accurate idea of what wilderness is, what kind of impacts threaten it, and what measures might protect it, than we did only a few decades ago. Wildland recovery projects headed up by thoughtful activists look like they will remain a viable part of our future landscape.

So this would be one in-between or bardo state: wilderness. Just as we exist in an interglacial period—the glaciers withdrew around 10,000 years ago but will surely descend as they follow earth's old rhythmic cycles—let's say we live in an inter-wilderness period. A fearsome bardo condition of loud painful flashes, wrenching cries, & conflicting images, where humans as a species have to determine how (and who gets) to live in the future.

One truism is that among species it is usually those at the top of the food chain that disappear first when the ecological fabric is torn. Big predators. So I've been happily intrigued by several animal recovery projects. All over North America one uninvited critter has been working diligently on its own recovery: the mountain lion (a.k.a. cougar, puma, catamount, painter). This grand cat has been reappearing in stable numbers here in the Southern Rocky Mountain Ecosystem where I live, also in California, Florida, and Vermont. In fact it never quite went away. Wolves, another strikingly beautiful predator, might therefor be better indicators of a true bardo stage. The gray or timber wolf was once the most widely distributed mammal on earth, including North America. Most of our lower forty-eight states, beginning with Massachusetts, hunted it to extinction. Henry David Thoreau watched New Hampshire residents torch Mt. Monadnock to clear out the wolf dens. And Colorado's last wild wolf was shot in 1945. Nonetheless several organizations have been working seriously on reintroducing the wolf to Colorado, led by the cheerfully non-bureaucratic activist group Sinapu (Ute Indian word for wolf). Already wolf populations have been returned successfully by the U.S. Forest Service, up north in Wyoming to Yellowstone. They have also reintroduced Mexican wolf populations to New Mexico, though down there success is still a question mark.

Various locations have been suggested for Colorado, topped by Rocky Mountain National Park and parts of the White River National Forest. Estimates say that the state could maintain about a thousand wolves off the "surplus" of deer and elk (those that don't make it through winter due to overpopulation). There is strong, reasonable opposition from ranchers, deer hunters, rural residents, and other people who are likely to run into wolves. These folk will have to be brought into the fold of course, in order for reintroduction to be a success. Yet public opinion appears to be overwhelmingly for reintroduction, and old superstitions, such as the dangers posed by wolves to human children, die out. My favorite bumper sticker reads: Little Red Riding Hood Lied.

I hold to a crazy belief that either myself & my friends, or my daughter & hers, will live to hear wolves howl once again in the Southern Rockies. Sometimes it seems inevitable. Listen hard as you will tonight, though, you won't hear them. Wolf was here, wolf went away. Will wolf return? We live in a planetary hell of lost mammals. But with some hard intelligent work—by eco-activists, biologists, game wardens, Buddhist practitioners, and poets— this might not have to be a hell for some notable species, but a bardo. An in between state.

Letter To BLM Area Manager
Levi Deike
(7 May 1999)

IN MAY 1999 *I received an e-mail alert from a consortium of environmental organizations about a proposed wrap of the Arkansas River by the artists Christo and
Jean-Claude. The artists' project, entitled "Over the River," would stretch perforated
sheets of translucent blue fabric at a heighth of 10-23 feet above the Arkansas river-
bed. Steel wire cables, anchored high on the river banks, are proposed to anchor the
panels of fabric. The project has been in the works a long time. Christo and Jean-
Claude drove through the Rocky Mountains with a group of friends and "collabora-
tors" in the month of August in 1992, 1993, and 1994. They claim to have logged
14,000 miles, "prospecting" eighty-nine rivers. The Rockies interested them because
they rightly noted that much United States water originates in the various watersheds of the Northern and Southern Rocky Mountains.*

*While something like twenty-eight agencies need to confer approval (partch-
work land ownership & politics of the American West), the BLM seems the key agency.
It is care-taker of the public lands along that stretch of the Arkansas, between Salida
and Cañon City. The Christos currently await approval on two projects—all this you
can check out on the various websites dealing with their proposed "wraps." Whichever
project receives approval first is the one they will turn their attention to. At the close of
their statements they send love to their supporters (whose reciprocal love of the artists
will help finance the project). Some of us eco-activists get a little grouchy hearing
about a project so likely to disrupt fragile eco-zones. Love for the eagles, kingfishers,
sand pipers, ducks, geese, and great blue herons dependent on the Arkansas might be
better demonstrated than by six miles of artificial fabric.*

*The following is a letter I wrote to then-Area Manager Levi Deike of the Bureau
of Land Management when I first heard of the Christo project.*

Dear Mr. Deike

I understand the artists Christo and Jeane-Claude have applied for a use permit for BLM land under your jurisdiction. Their proposal is to install an art project, a "wrap" of the Arkansas River between Cañon City and Salida, by winding a four or six mile curtain of fabric over the river. It will be anchored by cables bolted to the river banks and valley walls.

As an artist and resident of the state of Colorado, I am writing to urge you not to issue this permit. There are considerable reasons based on Arkansas River ecology to shut this thing down. As a landowner (I have a small piece of land higher up the watershed—near Trout Creek Pass), I can say that up here we consider bighorn sheep, pronghorn, black bear and elk rather important neighbors.

The bighorn in particular is a creature that's been badly stressed by human development throughout the Southern Rockies. Bighorn show what wildlife scientists call a "high degree of site fidelity." This means even under pressure they don't stray very far—they like their neighborhood. The banks of the Arkansas down to Cañon City are key habitat for them. Introduce heavy machinery, several days of blasting (needed to anchor Christo's diaphanous horizontal panels), as well as motorcades of art spectators, and local herds could be considerably affected. They easily get edgy and confused, which makes them susceptible to lungworm-pneumonia, principle killer of wild sheep in the Rockies.

The Arkansas River watershed through that canyon is also high altitude terrain and comparatively dry. As you know, a footprint or tire track stays on the ground a long time. Drilling into rock formations along the river banks or up on canyon walls in order to anchor support cables is going to produce scars and erosion problems that could last centuries. Thousands of curious spectators will also affect the ecology—aren't the artists speaking of several hundred thousand visitors? Changes in regular sunlight or wind patterns caused by miles of fabric, no matter how it's hung, are going to disrupt riverine ecology, the riparian plant communities, and any waterfowl that visit the area. I bet no ecologist has figured out what a curtain like that does to a river system, how if affects sunlight or local wind patterns.

When Christo drew a "curtain" across the valley near Rifle, unexpected winds quickly tore the fabric apart. Hours after it was hung, blaze orange scraps of nylon were blowing far down valley. What if something goes wrong near Salida? Six miles of soggy blue fabric in the Arkansas ain't going to look like good art.

Christo's proposal comes from a mind sadly unattuned to ecology. His installations—big, technological, and costly—may not seem out of place in a large city where the dominant structures are already human. I thought his wrap-up of the Pont Neuf in Paris looked rather tender. But bringing these monumental installations to non-urban landscapes, especially ones populated by threatened wildlife, is an act of colonialism not art. By colonialism, I mean when an outsider imposes an institution—economic, civic, governmental, artistic—in disregard of local interests. It is somewhat reminiscent of the enormously suspect and surely damaging water projects undertaken by the Bureau of Reclamation.

This Arkansas River art installation project is totally out of kilter with the regional economy; it ignores the habits of local folk—human, animal, fish, bird, plant. You've seen fierce local opposition thwart the proposed dam on the Arkansas, which would have given Colorado Springs water for burgeoning suburbs at the expense of an important watershed. Christo's proposal is comparable. He's willing to disrupt (if there's an accident, make that *destroy*) a major watershed drainage so he can temporarily set up an industrial project appreciated by international art-lovers in New York or Paris at the expense of the area's residents.

Don't think rejecting Christo a permit means right-wing fundamentalist anti-art Jesse Helms types win. Plenty of artists and writers these days are working at ecologically astute projects. At the Kerouac

School of Poetics in Boulder, Colorado, faculty have been articulating an ecologically balanced poetics and various innovative notions of bioregional poetry for two decades. Jack Collom, Joanne Kyger, Gary Snyder, Cecilia Vicuña, Anne Waldman, Ed Sanders, myself, a clutch of others have been figuring ways to put together art, based on a bit of local first-hand nature know-how. How about instead of Christo's "wrap" a modest poetry reading to celebrate local watersheds? We could show up in moccasins. . . .

Respectfully,
ANDREW SCHELLING
The Jack Kerouac School of Disembodied Poetics
Naropa University

Wandering Clouds
Buddhist Poet Monks of China

This essay originally served as the Introduction to The Clouds Should Know Me By Now: Buddhist Poet Monks of China, *edited by Red Pine and Mike O'Connor (Wisdom Publications: Somerville, 1998). The six translators include the editors, as well as Burton Watson, J.P. Seaton, Paul Hansen, and James Sanford.*

GNARLED PINES, WIND-BLOWN CLOUDS, jutting mountain pinnacles, exiled scholars, horses, trailing willows. Moonlight on meandering rivers, tiny fishermen, white cranes and mandarin ducks, the eerie screech of a gibbon, tiny white plum blossoms on twisted branches, a battered wooden boat moored in the distance. For more than a thousand years the poets of Buddhist China wandered a landscape that is vast and at the same time intimate, mysterious and deeply familiar: the same mountain peaks, the same agrarian villages, the same river gorges. What makes this landscape feel so much like home? The poets of China, many of them Ch'an (Zen) practitioners, had a way of quickly getting down to elemental things. Using a vocabulary of tangible, ordinary objects, they composed unsentimental poems that seem the precise size of a modest human life—the reflective sadness, the fleeting calm pleasures.

There exists a sizable amount of poetry written by Ch'an Buddhist poet-monks *(shih-seng),* men of enviable literary talent who lived out their years during turbulent times in accord with old Buddha's precepts. Their work spans 1100 years, from the middle T'ang dynasty until the opening years of the twentieth century. One or two have had a taste of renown in the West, on the basis of a couple of poems, but the rest have gone unheralded. Several were established Buddhist teachers of their own day, the influence of their subtle minds reaching deep, but they had little reputation as poets. Recognition of their literary efforts comes late. Only Chia Tao, the earliest of the poets translated here, did not devote his adult life to Buddhist monasticism. He slipped off the monk's "robe of patches" in his early thirties to pursue a life of poetry, which he supported with marginal government employment and years of inadequate pay. One lingers over the detail of his brief autobiography: at the time of his death his worldly possessions comprised a five-string zither and an ailing donkey. Chia Tao stuck by his decision to make poetry a life's path, but a whiff of regret sometimes lifts from his verse.

As Buddhists, these men traveled a great deal. Reading their poems you observe how deliberately they led, as Thoreau would put it, hyper-aetherial lives—"under the open sky." It is no accident then that a prevalent theme in the poetry is the farewell poem for a comrade, typically situated at daybreak after a night of wine or tea, vivid talk or silent companionship. These poets spent their days living in and journeying between the numerous Buddhist sites of pre-modern China—village temples, remote points of pilgrimage, monasteries tucked in the forest, the mountain yogin's hut secluded in a mossy gulch. Add to this Buddhist imperative to travel the simple fact that over the several millennia of recorded Chinese history, political and military events have been shifty and uncertain. Scholars, poets, civil servants, Buddhist abbots, even monks of no reputation, found themselves driven from region to region, forced into exile through windblown mountain passes, or when the regime shifted, recalled up a thundering river gorge to serve in some official capacity. Many of these journeys were memorialized in poems.

Mountains, forests, rivers—these make up the well known landscapes of Chinese painting. In the poetry a clipped, selective vocabulary, surprisingly ambiguous in the Chinese originals, merely suggests what's out there. It is left to the reader to fill in the details—tumbling watercourses, looming peaks, twisted mountain strata, lowland pools, deer and wild gibbons, wind-stunted trees. Always alongside the poet, non-human creatures move easily into the world of the poem. Deer and wild cranes may follow their own customary tracks, but their travels seem to meaningfully crisscross the poet's. At times untamed creatures become, with only a touch of irony, profound teachers for the wandering-cloud poets. By an interesting karmic twist, these various citizens of Chinese verse have in recent decades sensitized American readers to distinct features of our own continent: water-sheds and eco-zones, seasonal weather cycles, animal rutting habits, plant successions, and the like.

Not surprisingly, a disproportionate number of non-academic American translators have made their home in the Pacific Northwest states, where the natural world—its dark clutching forests, shy owls, concealing mists, abrupt icy pinnacles lit by a fugitive ray of sun—so resembles the setting of a Chinese poem. Across the centuries you can hear Chia Tao asking, "Where is the master? Gathering herbs, off on the mountain, hidden by clouds."

In China there was also a nature poetry of almost comic literalness: *shih-shu*, "rock-and-bark poetry." In 1703 a Buddhist poet even assumed this term for a nom de plum, and craftily hid his identity behind it. How widely the phrase circulated remains a matter of dispute for scholars, but *shih-shu* were colloquially written, mildly irreverent poems—poems not simply sceptical of city-folk hustle, or merely celebratory of reclusive hours spent in savage wilderness settings. Rather than being brushed on paper or silk, *shih-shu* were incised on scraps of bamboo, scratched into tree-bark and rocks, or pecked into cliff-faces. The notorious practitioner of this genre, maybe the originator of *shih-shu*, was poet Han-shan (possibly seventh century), known to American readers as Cold Mountain. Translations by R.H. Blyth, Gary Snyder, Red Pine, and Burton Watson have made Han-shan and his lively sidekick Shih-te well known in recent decades to North Americans.

According to Lu-ch'iu Yin, a minor T'ang government official and Buddhist enthusiast, Han-shan's *gāthā,* or Buddhist verse, were left littered around the forbidding cliff from which the poet took his name. The Han-shan promontory lies along the T'ien-t'ai range in Chekiang, a strikingly wild region in southern China. Contemporary photographs show cornfields beneath the rock wall, but in Han-shan's day the land was heavily forested, and local woodcutters or monks occasionally saw the poet disappear into a cave, which in some unsettling accounts would close up behind him.

Unable to coax Han-shan, a man he deeply admired, into establishing closer ties to the world of civilized people (Han-shan just giggled, threw stuff, and ran into the woods), the well-intended but rather unimaginative Lu-ch'iu Yin sent a troop of men into the mountains to collect what of the scattered poems they could find—about three hundred. The legend of ragged Han-shan and his equally eccentric comrade Shih-te became a reference for countless later poets, who saw in their cryptic behavior—as much as in their poetry—a deep Buddhist realization. In the 1960s, the California poet Lew Welch, much taken with Chinese scholar poems and the habits of Ch'an hermits, is said to have left the sole copy of one of his own poems tacked to a barroom wall in Sausalito.

The karma runs deep. In the late 1980s a group of American poets gathered one spring at Green Gulch Farm's Zen Center, twenty minutes by car north of Sausalito, to talk about poetry and Buddhist meditation. It marked the first time such an event had been convened east of the Bering Strait. Open to the public, the gathering hosted the usual cast of characters: blue-jean bodhisattvas, long-haired yogins, quick-witted yoginīs, nautch girls, coyote men, patch-robe monastics, and unemployed scholars. The gathering caught the echo of earlier events, "Ch'an guests and poetry masters," that by the eighth century had become regular practice in China.

That particular weekend, in a pond back of the drafty Green Gulch zendo, a frog sangha held its own convocation—like the gibbons and wild cranes of Chinese verse—while many good human remarks were made during the indoor conferences. One statement in particular has stuck with me. The poet-priest Norman Fischer in a very unsensational fashion said, "Meditation is when you sit down and do nothing. Poetry is when you sit down and do something." With these sage words he neatly wiped out centuries of debate—India, China, Japan—over whether poetry is a legitimate pursuit for the earnest Buddhist in search of realization.

Yes, meditation and poetry. Hard to imagine with what sobriety the early Buddhists in India enjoined monks and nuns against literary pursuits. It is equally striking that as late as the year 817 the renowned Po Chü-i could write:

> Since earnestly studying the Buddhist doctrine of emptiness,
> I've learned to still all the common states of mind.

Only the devil of poetry I have yet to conquer—
let me come on a bit of scenery and I start my idle droning.
(translation by Burton Watson)

Without doubt, these two distinctly human undertakings, making song
and watching mind, go inestimably far back into prehistory. Would contemporary North American consumer culture not offer a bemused smile
to the notion of a conflict between them? Aspirants watch out! Remember
Chia Tao's zither and old sick donkey! There seems so little time these days,
and hopelessly little reward, for practicing either. Yet a not-so-secret, and
surprisingly durable, counterculture keeps the two alive, evidently unable
to do without either. Often the two practices get pursued hand in hand, or,
as Norman Fischer noted, in nearly the same posture. Luckily, as North
Americans, we don't have to cut back too much growth in order to keep
the hall of practice clear. Behind us stand heartening documents from Asia,
compiled over the course of several thousand years, to show what others
have done.

Over the last few centuries, the poetry movements from continental
Europe, England, and America—movements or schools such as Romanti-
cism, Symbolism, Pre-Raphaelitism, Imagism, Futurism, Vorticism, Dada,
Surrealism, Mythopoetics, Fluxus, Language Poetry—have made powerful
breaks with the past. Poets needed to confront our disordered human
realm, its conflicts and anguish, to envision new social forms; and the work
has been heroically done. Yet there's relief when the poems of old China,
steeped in Buddhist or Taoist thought, come forward to point another path
through the modern world. Influenced by Buddhist and Taoist views of nature, Chinese poetry *(shih)* has helped invigorate an American poetry that's
willing to wander away from bustling human settlements and the urban
settings of most twentieth century verse. Yet the social impasses and ago-
nies, the stuff of being all-too-human, don't disappear; they simply move
for a moment into the moonlight when the Ch'an masters speak. And a
landscape suffused with Buddhist emptiness comes forth.

Poems of friendship, family life, travel; poems with a breath of pine
wind. They strike a tone that's seasoned, deeply and resolutely secular.

Honesty, hard luck, good humor, close friends, a taste for simple things, tea, wine, moonlight. From the point of view of Buddhist doctrine, these poems are "invisible." Philosophical meaning lies hidden in the landscape, back of the trees, out in the mist. Dogma or preachiness would make the poem impudent.

Wang Wei (701-761), a Buddhist practitioner and a careful student of landscapes, established a further quality of much Ch'an poetry: the exclusion of anything grand, sensational, strenuous, or heroic. It is a very particular yogic restraint for the poem, and leaves us with men (and a few women) that sound like they could be talking to us directly. Not preaching, singing, or thundering; just talking. Certainly they know disorder, war, cruelty, injustice—their grief is evident. Yet it's as though they think they can rectify things with a poetry that places little solitary humans in cloud-covered mountains. A sort of Outward Bound of literature?

Americans of many backgrounds, who not long ago admired and cultivated a lean, resolute character, were waiting for word of these traditions: the bitter tea of Ch'an Buddhism, poetry with the taste of gnarled wood. After all, how many among us learnt first poetry skills by rewriting some old Chinese poem? How many among us got a first taste of Zen by copying a detail out of the life of some Chinese hermit met in a book? Or saw an ink-brush scroll in which a thin stream drops from cloud-piercing pinnacles—then noticed a tiny pavilion, one quiet scholar gazing into the void—all done in a few confidant strokes?

It was not until 1915 that Chinese poetry reached the English speaking world in a memorable way. Working from handwritten notebooks of maverick art historian Ernest Fenollosa, Ezra Pound put together a group of seventeen Chinese poems and called it *Cathay*. Although the title looks backward, to a colonial period marked by British gunships and trade companies—"Cathay, and the Way Thither" —the collection of poems, mostly translations from T'ang poet Li Po's work, points to a future that would know Asia, not as an overseas continent to be plundered for spice and fiber, but as a homeland to writers of a poetry that reads like a product of our own time.

Pound published his book in London, midway through World War I. At the time, many of his close comrades were holding the trenches in France or Italy—Henri Gaudier-Brzeska, Wyndham Lewis, Richard Aldington, and Ernest Hemingway. Some would be dead, others wounded, before the war was over. It is no surprise, then, that his attention went to poems about war's human cost: boyish conscripts holding outposts against a formidable enemy, lonely girls who should have had lovers, honest scholars brushed into exile. His book still stands as one of the best. But there was a great deal more to Chinese poetry.

A large amount of Chinese poetry came to North America in the years after the Second World War, a golden age for verse and translation. Scholars and soldiers who had seen action in the Pacific theater brought back a bit of Asian culture. Kyoto in the mid-fifties developed a lively expatriate group of poets, translators, Zen students, and scholars. Young writers in the States, spurred to the modern flavor of *shih,* were able to book cheap passage to Asia by boat, or they journeyed there figuratively by staying home, drinking tea, and getting Chinese ideograms under their belts. One of the influential publications was Gary Snyder's translation of twenty-four Han-shan poems (1958), which thousands of Americans read. That same year Jack Kerouac's book *The Dharma Bums* gave Han-shan and Zen Buddhism the flavor of cultural revolution. "I see a vision of a great rucksack revolution, thousands or even millions of young Americans wandering around with their rucksacks, going up the mountains to pray, making children laugh and old men glad . . . Zen lunatics who go about writing poems." Ch'an Buddhist poets seemed right up to date.

What was so modern about the old poets? Kenneth Rexroth wrote of Tu Fu (712-770): "Tu Fu comes from a saner, older, more secular culture than Homer and it is not a new discovery with him that the gods, the abstractions and forces of nature, are frivolous, lewd, vicious, quarrelsome, and cruel, and only men's steadfastness, love, magnanimity, calm, and compassion redeem the nightbound world." He also said, "Tu Fu is not religious at all. But for me his response to the human situation is the only kind of religion likely to outlast this century. 'Reverence for life,' it has been called."

Reverence for life (Sanskrit *ahiṃsa:* non-injury, no wanton killing) was a cornerstone of Buddhist practice in India long before a few first sūtra lit-

eratures took the rugged northeast road into China, influencing Chi
and his poetry cohorts. Maybe we're in a position now to see that this is
what's so compelling in 1500 years of Ch'an poetry. The best poems push
no doctrine or dogma, there's no jingo, no prosyletizing. The Buddhism
is carefully hidden away in tight five and seven syllable lines. (This metric
pattern, according to Yunte Huang, "is intimately related to the translations from the Sanskrit Buddhist texts. It was the encounter with an al-
phabetical language—Sanskrit—that made the Chinese realize for the
first time that a Chinese character was pronounced by a combination of
vowel and consonant.") There it lurks—archaic and instantly modern—a
reverence for life: one's own, one's companions, one's fellow earth-
dwelling creatures.

Ezra Pound compiled a book of Li Po's verse while young men across
Europe were fighting in trenches. It seems he conceived *Cathay* as an anti-
war book, not propaganda, but as the effort a poet might make in order to
shift the way people see things. Why is it that behind the stolid, often melancholy tone of so much Chinese verse—a tone long ago admiringly called
"bland, like the taste of withered wood"—modern ears detect an acute
comradeship with all forms of life? Nearly as far back as Chinese literature
goes occurs the term *the ten thousand things,* Taoist shorthand for the planet's
numberless creatures. "Sentient beings are numberless, I vow to save them,"
goes the chant in the zendo. This camaraderie, or instant sense of warm-
heartedness, is what makes such a contribution to Buddhist literature, to
ecology ethics, and to postmodern poetry.

Chia Tao—   The solitary bird
                       loves the wood;
                       your heart also
                       not of this world.

Ch'i-chi—   On my pillow little by little waking,
                       suddenly I hear a single cicada cry—
                       at that moment I know I have not died

Pao T'an—

Frosty wind
Raises deep night,
Missing only
A gibbon's howl.

Han-shan Te-ch'ing—

Who can be like wild deer on deserted
mountains
satisfied with tall grass and pines

Shih-shu—

my heart is free as the white clouds
body light as crimson leaves
apes and birds pull me forward

Ching An—

White clouds too know the flavor
of this mountain life

Dōgen Zenji, the thirteenth-century Japanese philosopher versed in Ch'an practice, picked up the spirit in his own cranky, mischievous way—

That the self advances and confirms the ten thousand things
is called delusion;
That the ten thousand things advance and confirm the self
is called enlightenment.

There is good testimony that long familiarity with meditation— months, years, decades—contributes to a person's clear-headedness, focus, and good humor. Past such personal benefits, it's also possible you become a better citizen. A heightened sense of empathy seems to emerge— one that even crosses the boundaries between nature's "kingdoms," human, animal, insect, or plant. Tibetan Buddhists vow to liberate all beings, down to "the last blade of grass," and ecologists of many persuasions are currently studying, naming, and yes, vowing to save (often with the assistance of enlightened legislation like the Endangered Species Act) a last blade of grass.

Perhaps there was an era when poetry didn't pay much attention to these things. But if the ecologists are right, we currently dwell in a period the future will know as "the great dying." Edward O. Wilson and a range of other accomplished scientists have produced hard and compelling evidence that we little humans are bringing about the fastest wave of species extinction known in the four-billion-year history of our blue-green planet. Maybe one of the consciousness-shifting tools we humans can use if we hope to turn this around are the poems left by departed Chinese masters. I expect it will be the poems of invisible Buddhist insight, wrapped in mist or moonlight, pulsing with a quiet compassion, and not the poems of an expressly doctrinal character, that will give us the best bearing.

So take a walk with the Ch'an buddha-ancestors, these cranky, melancholy, lonely, mischievous poet-ancestors. Their songs are stout as a pilgrim's stave or a pair of good shoes, and were meant to be taken on the great journey. Even Han-shan Te-ch'ing—who ruined his legs from prolonged zazen and needed someone to carry him to his teapot, his writing table, his gate, or his window—even he wrote poetry that flies with the cranes, crisscrosses the slopes with the deer, drifts with the white clouds. If it all seems ordinary to you, well, it should. Whoever said poetry, or an abiding companionship with deer and wild cranes, were anything unusual?

Tyger Tyger

THE SMALL OUTFIT of contemporary techno-wizards who've taken up digs at The House of William Blake had some Americans by for a visit in May. Seventeen South Molton Street—last standing residence where William and Catherine Blake lived. The neighborhood's pricey these days, the global economy whirrs past its door, and sharply outfitted women go hunting for clothes. *Milton* and *Jerusalem* got written in second floor rooms, a sizable hand press stood by the window that fronts the street.

The good people in residence at the Blake house have almost no relics, but they did bring out a single archival box—stencils for *Milton*—also showed us wide modern drafting tables and high-end computer monitors used like bellows and anvil for angelic techno-designs out of Hell. Biscuits sat by the firebox where Blake once burnt coal. There was wine and a white British cheese. Warmed by the hospitality of our gentle hosts, and considering that the tiger Blake observed at the London Zoo had been brought out of India, I reframed a stanza of "Tyger" to Sanskrit. Had nobody tried it before? Surely some ganja-headed pundit of old Bengali renaissance days—?

> śārdūla śārdūla ratrivaneśu
> tejāḥ prajvalan
> ko 'mrtaḥ hasto va chakṣu va
> te bhīmaṃ rūpaṃ kartuṃ śaknoti

Early June, home to the Colorado foothills, west by a tiger's hair of the 105th Meridian. Icy mist holds the Front Range. It crawls down from the summits through boulder-choked canyons, leaving needles of frost on dark Douglas fir. Evening it vanishes upwards. Red Dakota hogbacks slip forth, a glimpse of smoky forest ravines that drop from Indian Peaks. Then precipice moon.

Who wandered these forests when Blake was setting Tyger to verse?
Ute Indians mostly. A few tough Frenchmen out trapping beaver.
And *did he smile his work to see?*

The region's dominant cat is *Felis concolor*—cougar, catamount, puma—mountain lion or painter—depends where in N. American space you picked up your speech. A Tupi Indian word passed to French trappers. Or archaic Greek, bent to the way things get said Upper South.

painter : panther : *Panthera tigris*

Caught in a coyote snare
       on the Uncompahgre plateau,
I saw you there
thy tawny pelt
thy pelt philosophic & tattered
       thy stiff drying deer-color'd pelt—

Blake died in 'twenty-five. Five years earlier, Dr. Edwin James went up Blue Cloud Summit, botanizing the tundra, and named the mountain for Zebulon Pike. In '06 Pike had gone through and put cat tracks into his army report. By which time Blake had turned upside down a full notebook, and was drafting Tyger and London on the same empty page. The Southern Rockies were still Louisiana—blank on maps in the London cartographer shops.

Hail catamount,
tawny end-of-tail flicker once glimpsed as the
mesa grass stirr'd,
or felt dread feet when the stars
threw down their spears over high twilit
meadow alone—?

A scrape of dirt & debris, whiff of sharp urine
muddy track in the gloam.
Lay it down Tyger Tyger for humans—
& frame old symmetries
        new poems.

Joanne Kyger's Portable Poetics

28 July 1997 / Pátzcuaro

In the dream Donald and Joanne show up. We're delighted they've joined us in Patzcuaro. But inside a barroom full of local handcrafted objects we find a cabinet of colorful Michoacán shelves loaded with science fiction body-snatcher pods. The pods are intricately lacquered with blue and white Indian designs. It seems they've been put here to replace humanity. An apocalyptic mood settles over the room. Joanne departs for the mercado to buy ceramic cups—"cupitos" she calls them—leaving me and Donald to figure out the immense complicated coffee machine while Anne keeps vigil over the pods. Someone's put the machine together wrong. When I throw a switch it steams dangerously and coffee drizzles from many unpredictable valves.

I HAVE SEEN JOANNE KYGER over the past ten years in various temporary lodgings here in Boulder, and recently down in Mexico's Michoacán mountains. It was in January, in Pátzcuaro, that I asked about her principles for packing—how she gets it together to travel—and she told me she learnt a great deal in the sixties watching Gary Snyder pack his rucksack for the woods. Joanne moves into her quarters with modest duffel bag and backpack, and from it produces all manner of practical items, ritual objects, and writing tools. Up goes a portable Buddhist altar, small thangka painting tacked to the wall, and various select bandanas come unrolled. (She seems to have made a study of the many designs available, both north and south of the border, commenting on new patterns she encounters. I was unaccountably pleased recently when she asked me to teach her the knot I use for tying bandanas around the throat cowboy style—able to give back some bit of practical learning to one who has made a deep study of these things.) On and around the variety of bandanas go plates, spoons, knives; fruit from the local market, a flower or two, and a little larder of food chosen for quality and inexpensiveness. Tequila or beer; and tiny drinking cups, the "cupitos" that made it into the dream, she has picked up for pennies in Pátzcuaro's Friday open-air pottery market.

These details are not meant to be merely personal or anecdotal. I put them down because I've maybe learnt about how she writes as much from watching her travel habits as querying her poems on the page. Joanne Kyger is after all the preeminent living poet of the journal or notebook—old nearly underground tradition I like to trace back to Japan, where the *nikki* (day book) has survived as a durable genre for over a thousand years. A genre that seems to have been designed for the traveler.

The fine early journal practitioners in Japan were women of the Heian court (tenth and eleventh century). While the cultivated men were distracting themselves writing poems in classical Chinese, and remained dependent on large non-portable libraries, the courtesans were forging a peerless literary tradition based on the diary form. Direct observation and colloquial recording of events, people, places visited; conversations overheard; accounts of poetry competitions; as well as enough solid ethnography & natural history to make the period utterly vivid. After Arthur Waley's partial translation of Sei Shonagon, and then Ivan Morris's full version of *The Pillow Book* into English, the twentieth century had to hand a splendid up-to-date model for list poems of everything from trees and birds to "despicable things" and harsh sounding words. Other good diaries from the period are those of Murasaki Shikibu, the poet Izumi Shikibu, Lady Sarashina, the anonymous author of *The Gossamer Years,* and that of Lady Nijjo.

In the spirit of Basho who wrote "the journey itself is home," Joanne once told me: "Traveling, the journal is your home away from home, the place you live. The little book is your *casa*." And she continued with what everyone knows but needs to hear again, repeatedly—how in that book, in the domestic space of that casa, one ought to give things the dignity of their names. Such a practice in our planetary house of course implies a great scholarly interest directed towards the world. Go out and learn it all: birds, trees, landscapes, people, languages, customs, food, the prices travelers pay and the prices for locals. Get these things down while they are close to hand.

It is in her very important *Japan & India Journals* (reprinted under the title *Big Strange Moon*) that Joanne Kyger most fully (in terms of number of pages and timespans and regions covered) shows herself a terrifically disciplined yet sprightly & loosely omnivorous journal writer. Of the lessons one learns or somehow picks up over the years, for life & for poetry, only a handful really stand out. It was she who passed on to me one of the most serviceable: that the journal as a regular writing practice shifts the focus of writing from that old Occidental head trip "who are you"—to "when" and "where" are you. These questions it turns out are more interesting points for writing and living to proceed from. The writer's mindstream is freed on the instant, and can assume a relaxed and ironic removal from the inward junk of fluctuating mood intricacies; attention relocates on an out-there world: history, geopolitical observations, bioregional specifics like flora & fauna & weather currents, other peoples' customs, foreign vocabularies, and the indelible impact of capital on the twenty-first century.

Pátzcuaro for instance is a where. A *when* might take note: winter, the dry season, vegetation a little withered by drought; six years after Mexico's Zapatista insurgency put the PRI (government party) on notice and delivered around Mexico and into Michoacán a certain long-suppressed pride for the indigenos. Four hundred fifty years after the Jesuits constructed the first Western Hemisphere college (it's up on the hill near the Basilica, today used as a museum of regional folk life). Over at Plaza Chiquita is bronze statue of revolutionary hero Gertrudis Bocanegra baring her breasts to the firing squad: who's revolution and when? what was the legacy? why alongside Pátzcuaro's open air mercado and across from the biblioteca?

And so, one always enters the date, the time, and the location at the top of your entry. Notice how Kyger's poetry of recent decades follows suit, bringing this information to the bottom of the page, making of it a frame for the poem. There is something ceremonial in heading your page with where and when: it anchors what follows, if only a single word or thought. Not surprisingly, this is the advice found in bird-watch journals, back country notebooks, and has been used by most travelers of the hundred literary epochs. Anyone who goes on a journey, or takes an interest in ecology, bioregionalism, or that enormous journey of everything around us termed natural history, can't do with a better teaching.

Possibly Kyger's low-impact lifestyle and the way she packs and travels should go into some future handbook of how as a human being to dwell on our planet: lightly and with good bright humor. Beware enterprises requiring new clothes. But always put in your rucksack a clean notebook.

A Bioregional Poetry Class at Naropa

In 1997 I received *a Nathan Cummings Contemplative Fellowship, administered by the American Council of Learned Societies, to design and teach an undergraduate class at The Naropa Institute (now Naropa University) that would explore a three way link between poetry, bioregional studies, and contemplative practice. The intention was to see how yogic disciplines and traditional Asian arts might guide aspiring writers toward a nature literate and ecologically sensitive method of reading and writing poetry. Field trips and opportunities for reading and writing outside the classroom seemed essential. I wanted class readings to include both contemporary poetry and older verse traditions. Books on the syllabus: Lorine Niedecker's* The Granite Pail; The Essential Haiku *edited and mostly translated by Robert Hass; and Jerome Rothenberg's* Technicians of the Sacred: A Range of Poetries from Africa, America, Europe & Oceania. *Additional essays and poems came from Joanne Kyger, Arthur Sze, Kenneth Rexroth, H. D. Thoreau, Mary Austin, Leslie Silko, Jack Turner, Lao Tzu and others.*

Odd to note, beginning this essay, that the automatic word spell on a recently purchased (August, 2000) Microsoft Word 98 program accepts neither bioregion nor bioregionalism as recognizable words and underscores them with a jagged red line. The first North American Bioregionalist Congress was held in 1984. The American Heritage Dictionary (Third Edition, 1991) defines bioregion: "An area constituting a natural ecological community with characteristic flora, fauna, and environmental conditions and bounded by natural rather than artificial borders."

For some years I have searched for an adequate title for the kind of poetry I want to investigate in class. Nature poetry *I find useless as a term since commonly cited modern examples generally cling to painfully out-dated, neo-Victorian assumptions about both self and nature. Seasoned in airless creative writing workshops they announce greeting card sentiments, not innovative explorations of the poetic craft. My colleague at Naropa, Jack Collom, uses the term* Eco-Lit: *fine so long as nobody suppose it refers to a type of literature distinct from other genres. What could be less ecological? The phrase* bioregional poetry *I find awkward but perhaps serviceable. The advantage is that it implies a poetry rooted in direct experience of the immediate ecological community, with a view to how humans have adapted to and altered it over long stretches of time.*

So, a poetry that might learn from earlier models including those of pre-literate cultures, which often included richly developed lore regarding geophysical features of the landscape, flora, fauna, watersheds, and so forth. I could draw examples from much of ancient & classical Asia, parts of the pre-colonial tribal world, with some surprise appearances from old Europe. My hope: that this would be a poetry also in sympathy with Modernist and postmodern dicta: Imagist, Objectivist, New American Poet, and other 20th century avant gardes. Bioregionalism assumes an implicit politics: local & globally cognizant, anarchic & decentralized, counseling restraint in any approach to resources local or planetary.

So a brief sketch of a few activities explored in class. To establish the order of paragraphs as well as the subject list for investigation that concludes the piece, I used chance operations inspired by ideas drawn from Charles Darwin, Yoko Ono, and John Cage.

September '98

Each member of the class brings a local field guide. It takes thirty minutes to climb a lowlying mesa which gives a west-looking view into the Colorado Front Range. A grove of Ponderosa pines with some flat boulders provides the shaded, comfortable classroom. Small prickly pear cactus squat in the piedmont grasses below. High above on a hogback of the Dakota formation juts the distinct rock formation Devil's Thumb. The human eye moves along the ridge, taking in views of notorious & technical local climbs: The Maiden, Jamcrack Spire, Mountains of the Moon. Slightly to the south stands The Matron, another guidebook climb, spookily resembling a terracotta Madonna. After compiling a list of local plant, bird, and animal species identified on the way up the Towhee Trail (Rufous-sided towhee everywhere evident with its distinctive chup chup chup zeeeeeee), the group carefully reads Lorine Niedecker's poem "Wintergreen Ridge," eyes narrowed on how she wove details of Wisconsin natural and human history into the poem.

There is the trail sign she cobbled in—

> *Flowers*
> > *loveliest*
> > > *where they grow*

> *Love them enjoy them*
> > *and leave them so*

A photograph of the original sign appears in Jenny Penberthy's *Niedecker:Woman & Poet*. No reason to think it's not still there, maintained by the pre-Environmental-movement local women who saved Wisconsin's Wintergreen Ridge from bulldozers: "we want it for all time." The poem suggests a rural, activist presence on the ecology front well before the advent of Earth First! or Greenpeace. Here, by the Colorado trailhead where today's climb started, a Park Service board offers a trove of colorful local names in Whitmanic fashion and announces trail closures meant to preserve raptor bird nests. Other postings alert human visitors to presence of mountain lion and, since this is autumn, bear foraging the low country in search of serviceberry and chokecherry.

Quick calibration to the reconstructed "Calendar from the Upper Paleolithic" in *Technicians of the Sacred* finds these initial class meetings fall between Moon of the Nut and Moon of the First Frost. A piece of reindeer leg-bone scored with lunar phrasings. The current assignment, more than twenty millennia after that Siberian calendar was dropt on the ice, is for each student to devise their own calendar, calibrated to a childhood bioregion. November's full moon, which will serve as occasion for the collective reading and writing of renga ("linked-verse" collaborative poems) outdoors on the Naropa campus, possibly in early snow, possibly under an edgy Chinook wind, will rise over the traffic light on Arapahoe Avenue.

The time frame of "Wintergreen Ridge" (call it the fiction): it runs the course of an afternoon's walk. Comparable to the three hour cut of time in which a Naropa University poetry-class field-trip takes place. It is Niedecker's longest poem. The deliberation and patience which she famously applied to her poetry suggest the poem would have been devised over a long stretch of time. Notes compiled on a two hour walk in an old-fashioned dress—

            an inch below

        the knee
            the style before
            the last

—then labored over for how many weeks? "Two months on six lines of poetry" the wry disclosure of her habit in another poem. Quotes and references throughout: D.H. Lawrence, Linnaeus, Charles Darwin, Henry James's father, T. S. Eliot, Niedecker's own contemporary and friend Basil Bunting. This means research at home—even a class of ten doesn't carry that many books on a hike. Items from the local paper get worked into the tight stanzas. Specific plants grow riotously through, their Linnaean classifications, careful visual descriptions, anecdotes, jokes (yes, plants exchange jokes), and life cycles. A mix of wild & garden variety flora, native & introduced, spread along the ambling three-steps-then-a-brief-pause form of her poem: *pipsissewa*.

Before starting down the class ambled across to the south rim of the mesa (startling a mule deer from its bed in a thicket). As counterpoint to any tendency towards naïve or overly romanticized views of ecology, which might avoid the planet's current problems and crises, we took on an investigative poetics study of the bioregion's single most alarming issue: the former Department of Energy plutonium trigger factory at Rocky Flats. There it sits, three miles through thin air, behind a few experimental energy windmills: a string of obsolete cinderblock buildings on a low mesa. The high rises of Denver protrude like crystals from behind the industrial complex, seventeen miles downwind and downwater. From 1953-1989 this "machine shop" produced triggers for the nation's nuclear arsenal. Plutonium manufactured at the Hanford site in Washington state arrived by rail or road at Rocky Flats, to be manufactured into "pits," the fissionable plutonium triggers that detonate a uranium weapon. Currently the site is being dismantled, the formidable laboratories taken carefully apart at enormous public expense. Over the past ten years the site's name has mutated, first to the cheerfully optimistic Rocky Flats Environmental Technology Site, then to the decisive Rocky Flats Closure Project. Can you hold a book of poetry against the electric security fence.

Early October

On trails throughout the Rocky Mountain foothills one notices ubiquitous *sign* of *Ursus americanus*, the North American black bear: berry laden scat. Advice on what to do if menaced by a large mammal is differently given by Park Service postings for each species. "If threatened by a bear play dead." "If attacked by a mountain lion fight back."

"No matter what the weather" haiku discussion & writing takes place—along with afternoon tea—in a rocky outcropping in Long Canyon, buried in Douglas fir trees on the flanks of Green Mountain. Topic: the distinctive styles of Bashō, Buson, and Issa, sometimes referred to by Japanese critics as exemplifying in their verse religion, art, and life, respectively. The hiss of a primus stove for Japanese *sencha* tea, the study of insects on the forest floor; examining the precepts of Basho that his students transcribed into notebooks and which give to us, at the edge of the twenty-first century, a taste of his conversation in workshops. "The bones of *haikkai* are plainness and oddness." Haiku is outdoor activity because the goal is: make the universe your companion.

Since haiku accommodates itself to the seasons and works in collaboration with other arts (flower arrangement, calligraphy, music, painting, tea) the class makes a formal visit the following week to the Japanese tea house situated on Naropa's campus. You rinse your hands with bamboo ladle at a stone basin, deposit shoes outside, and enter the tiny pitch-roof building through a three foot door: humility. The tea master, Shoshana, has studied the art under Japanese masters representing several lineages. Her style is hybrid but cleanly etched into a sequence of formal gestures as she directs her guests in ritual drinking: how to sit cross-legged on the tatami mats, how to bow with both hands flat out before you, the delicate courtesies of the asymmetrical drinking bowl. This is a "relaxed" session, okay to talk and ask questions, discuss the history of tea, muse on its shared aesthetic with haiku. How many haiku precepts of Matsuo Bashō (1644-1694) can you link to Rikyu's Way of Tea? A leaf green powder smelling faintly of fresh straw, whisked into hot water with bamboo until frothy. That funny crab-like shuffle in a swishing kimono across the tatami mat to serve it. "Forgive me for drinking before you."

> There is a common element permeating Saigyō's lyric poetry, Sōgi's linked verse, Sesshu's painting, and Rikyu's tea ceremony. It is the poetic spirit (furabo), the spirit that leads one to follow nature and become a friend with things of the seasons.
>
> —Bashō

In the *tokonoma* (altar niche in the wall) a tiny flower arrangement is traditional—usually a nosegay or single flower plucked from a nearby garden and set off-kilter in a mute-colored vase. Or a piece of poetry casually dashed in black ink onto a short rice paper scroll to set the seasonal tone. The little brazier, the cast iron kettle. The tea master explains that the five elements, water, wood, metal, fire and air must all be represented.

Now, what species occurring in the haiku anthology can be found in our own bioregion? "A crow / has settled on a bare branch— / autumn evening." Everyone saves the rice paper square from their ceremonial tea sweet—bean paste or sesame—also coordinated to the season. Traditional following the ceremony to write a haiku on it and return it in gratitude. The following week the class provides the tea master a dozen haiku for her tokonoma.

Poets go pawing over shopworn mythologies, and neglect the grand drama of ecology, the great epic of evolution (Aldo Leopold). And so we move towards chance operation in Darwin, Thoreau, the Surrealists, the Fluxus outfit of sixties New York. Or collaboration, as in renga, the early Japanese form of eco-poetics: a hundred linked verses, written by a party of up to a hundred poets, which move through a complete cycle of the seasons. Careful guide-lines dictate when the full moon appears, where an erotic verse, at what juncture a change of locale. Each participant in a group-writing of renga brings a medicine bag full of previously composed *hokku*, "opening verse" of three brief lines, to the party, hoping one might be selected by the group to open the renga. These little opening verses were the origin of haiku. Under scrutiny a haiku must hold a single vivid bioregional detail.

Late October

Once upon a time the people of North America, along with citizens of other parts of the planet, fell prey to a mass hysteria. This condition was known as the Cold War. It produced, on a continent known for enormous natural splendor, one nation's nuclear arsenal. Rocky Flats stands out there on its mesa, one troubling reminder for our Southern Rocky Mountain bioregion of a threat that reaches into the distant future. Rocky Flats is a sig-nal landmark along I-25, The Nuclear Highway, which stretches from nuclear testing sites in southern New Mexico, past the laboratories of Los Alamos, past the NORAD command center at Cheyenne Mountain, and on up to the missile silos sunk in the high plains of Wyoming. Given this troubling ribbon of asphalt that runs the continent's spine, what role might a poet take? Walt Whitman sang the body electric. Is it now the body radioactive?

This question sits like a brooding gremlin alongside Jerome Rothenberg's notion, in *Technicians of the Sacred*, that the shaman (tribal in-dividual charged with redressing individual & social imbalance) stands as the archaic figure behind the poet. "Physician & custodian of the soul." The poem a central element in the medicaments? Able to restore a condition of health to the individual or social body? Or is it sadly out-dated to think the poet could redress the threat of war or nuclear annihilation with a poem? Rothenberg cites Eliade: "the fundamental data of human existence, that is, solitude, danger, hostility of the surrounding world."

On a dark, windy afternoon, a high security tour—two vans linked by walkie-talkie, since no one without authorization can leave the van and no van is to be out of touch with central security. First we wind along dirt roads of the 6000 acre buffer zone & examine (through closed windows) the ecological community. This portion of the front range of the Southern Rockies has been off-limit to developers for half a century and maintains a rare short grass / long grass prairie ecology. The site biologist provides species distribution maps.

Federal Special-Concern Species
with Potantial Habitat at Rocky Flats

Bell's Twinpod
Tulip Gentian
Adder's Mouth Orchid
Regal Fritterary
Plains Topminnow
Western Snowy Plover
Black Tern
Spotted Bat
Long-eared Myotis
Fringed Bat
Long-legged Myotis
Pale Townsend's Long-eared Bat
Plains Spotted Skunk
Swift Fox

The vans then thread past a security checkpoint and into the heavily guarded "industrial core," watched over by the largest private security force in Colorado. Wind kicks up dust—everyone here knows the place should have been called Windy Flats—and in the west, clouds lower through the Eldorado Springs gap. At the site of Tent 1 a backhoe is scraping the soil gingerly, along a trench where a hundred unidentified drums of contaminated material were recently found. The first drum disinterred— several weeks ago—alarmingly began to smoke. The diggers re-buried it in haste.

Lacking the Old Irish "Breastplate Against Death" of our anthology, or some similar charm, a few students have swallowed iodine pills.

> Bury the skull of a yak.
> Bury the skull of a black bitch.
> Hide the skulls of a dog & a pig under a child's bed, or bury a
> weasel's skull there, or a puppy's, or a piglet.
> Set out or bury the skulls of a fox, a badger, & a marmot in a
> cemetery.
> Bury the heads of a fish & of an otter.
>   (Tibet)

Rocky Flats. Fourteen point two (14.2) metric tons of plutonium, six to eight metric tons weapons-grade uranium. Reports of missing plutonium turn up with alarming regularity in the local papers, though the Department of Energy speculates most of it may be found in the ventilation system as workers continue to dismantle the buildings and figure out what to do with the "waste." Naturalist Peter Warshall once told a group at Naropa, "It is not waste. You cannot throw it away. You cannot dispose of it."

Plutonium will be deadly long after the glaciers have returned to carve up these mountains, long after the glaciers have gone north again. Plutonium's half life—the point at which half its radioactive isotopes have decayed—is 26,000 years. About the length of time back to the earliest Aurignacian cave paintings in Europe. About the range Jerome Rothenberg's anthology suggests for poetry, drawing a spiral line from Upper Paleolithic lunar notations found in Siberia to the Internet poets of today.

In 1969 the "costliest industrial fire in history" occurred at Rocky Flats, though the fire never breached the outer walls of the cinderblock building. Our guide referred to Building 771, where plutonium was once recovered from out-moded weaponry, as the most dangerous building in America. Congress wants all plutonium and other contaminants shipped off-site, and has currently re-calibrated the plant's closure date to the year 2006. At which point the buffer zone will revert to open space, the industrial core should be sheathed under a concrete pad, and dozens of plant and animal species—many of them with metabolisms and behavior patterns virtually unknown to humans—can slowly pursue their old contract with life.

"Please enjoy your cup of tea."

Investigation Topics / Bioregional Poetry
(for performance)

---

natural history the antidote to human vanity / Gregory Bateson
half life of plutonium
phenology: periodic shifts in flora and fauna due to seasonal changes
classical Tamil landscape poetics
plainness
vegetable eye (Blake)
settlement patterns & town names along the Platte, the Arkansas,
    the Rio Grande
Ikebana
global positioning system
diabolism in Western place names
Japanese crow poem
collage / cut ups / lists / collaboration
metabolism: the invisible spheres
Earth Liberation Front
eco-feminism
exquisite corpse / renga
postmodernism inherently ecological / no single viewpoint
transparency / opacity
those who rule the symbols rule us / Burroughs
sudden vs. gradual enlightenment
Indian Peaks
chance operation the method for evolution
vegetable soup or duck stew / Basho
daily journal practice / Thoreau

composition of lists & "filling the notebook with odd facts"
    / Sei Shonagon
mining, timber, ranching, tourism, hi-tech: economic succession
can Wilderness exist in a world with cell phones (philosophy)
lonesome traveler
Classical Sanskrit poetry's calibration of plants & animals to
    "the permanent emotions"
lore & language of schoolchildren / playground songs
Megafauna extinction North America during late Pleistocene
vegetation map for local watersheds
high cost of living drives students from the Front Range
animals as human / vs. Olson's human as animal
"The history of the lyric twitters and clucks with the transliteration of
    bird songs" (Lyn Hejinian)
many ways to go about making a work of art
does Ethnopoetics over-privilege shamanism to the neglect of ordinary
    life (women, children)
courting songs, marriage songs, work songs, lullabies, nursery rhymes,
    protest songs, the Blues
wilderness not in the past but the future
Zen art of Japan
biotechnology
Treaty of Guadalupe Hidalgo
mountain highways follow Indian trade routes
Sinapu / wolf reintroduction to Southern Rockies
haiku, tea, & the seasons
animals wander from one watershed to another plants generally don't
    "the bear went over the mountain"
rapid extinction of human languages an ecological concern
plutonium guardianship project / Joanna Macy
full moon poetry writing party
"Do not despise the green jewel among the leaves / because it is
    a traffic light." (Reznikoff)

mountains & rivers means Nation / China
botanical index: Thoreau, Ramanujan's Tamil anthology, ethnobotany
Notebook is medicine bag
wild plums, scarlet sumac / autumn in the foothills

Gazetteer

In a pocket notebook, quick directions
scrawled down in haste—
Devil's Gulch Road to Twin Owl Camp.
A stab of hunger at every word.
Who saw Bighorn below Dunraven peak?
Heard the elk mewling near Never Summer at dusk?
Was it silver and beaver pelt they hankered for
the men, mostly unschooled, who came down the Platte?
They wove a landscape.
Cow Creek or Cache la Poudre,
Rio de las Animas Perdidas en Purgatorio.
(*River of Souls Lost in Purgatory?*
Did they detect other tongues that got in before them?)
The United States are themselves the greatest poem, wrote Whitman,
and stanzas ring out like coins—

    Bighorn Flats

        The Needles

Hell's Hip Pocket

          Kawuneeche Valley

    Medicine Bow Curve

          Echo Creek

"These too are unrhymed poetry."

Mountain King
(ink on silk, Yi Dynasty, Korea)
Collection of Emille Museum, Seoul, Korea

In Korea, the tiger has been painted to chase away ill luck.
The tiger's ferocious strength is believed to be powerful enough
to ward off all evil influences. The tiger is the symbolic wild animal
of Korea, but also subject of folk tales similar to Native American
Coyote stories. Sometimes tiger gets to be ferocious and scare everyone
and sometimes magpie just laughs at such an idiotic creature or
rabbit pulls another fast one. Humor is given a strong expression in
Korean folk painting, *minhwa,* which reflects the experience of
observation and camaraderie in nature. Tiger is also the messenger
of the Mountain Spirit—what animates everything all at once,
everywhere, a humble faith in original, basic mystery.

COLOPHON

Set in Perpetua, designed by Eric Gill for Monotype (1925)
and named after the first book for which it was used—
The Passion of Perpetua and Felicity. An early participant in the
Arts & Crafts Movement, Gill was originally a stone-cutter
and letterer using his skills from tombstone cutting to
sign-painting. Pacifist, socialist, and social critic, Gill always
regarded himself foremost as a workman with a deep concern
for the integration of craftsmanship and industry. This typeface
is widely regarded as one of his best—small in x-height with
a strong, compact appearance and sprightly individuality.

•

Book design by J. Bryan

ANDREW SCHELLING, born January 14, 1953 in Washington D.C., grew up in the townships west of Boston. Early influences were the Northeast's resurgent conifer forests and granite faced mountains, its Transcendentalist heritage (Thoreau country), and Asian art collections seen in Boston and Cambridge museums. Moving west in 1973 he spent seventeen years in Northern California. Wilderness exploration, companionship with urban poets of the San Francisco Bay Area, and South Asian language studies at U.C. Berkeley. With Benjamin Friedlander he edited the poetics journal *Jimmy & Lucy's House of "K."* In 1990 he moved to Boulder, Colorado, where he joined the faculty of The Jack Kerouac School of Disembodied Poetics at Naropa University. He teaches poetry, Sanskrit, and bioregional writing. Schelling translates poetry from Sanskrit and related Indic vernaculars. In 1992 he was awarded The Academy of American Poets translation award and has received two grants from the Witter Bynner Foundation for Poetry. He lives in Boulder, along the ponderosa pine foothills of the Southern Rocky Mountains.